Workbook

Business Studies

David Floyd

Contents

Our economy

Inside and outside the business

People in business

Finance in business

Making the products

Selling the products

Exam practice

Homework diary

Topic	Score
Our economy	/36
Types of economy	/34
Locating business	/28
The European Union	/37
International business	/36
Sole trader and partnership businesses	/30
Limited companies	/34
Other businesses	/33
Stakeholders in business	/33
The main functions of business	/32
Organising business	/30
Communicating in business	/39
How a business grows	/34
Supporting business	/33
Business and the law	/33
Other influences on business	/35
Employing staff	/31
Training and developing staff	/35
Theories on motivating staff	/35
Paying staff	/35
Groups in business	/35
Working together	/35
Finance for business	/41
Financial records in business 1	/38
Financial records in business 2	/37
Interpreting business accounts 1	/29
Interpreting business accounts 2	/43
Costs in business	/44
Breaking even in business	/36
Budgeting in business	/34
Production in business	/37
Economies of scale	/43
Productivity	/33
Quality and stock control	/39
Marketing in business	/48
Market research	/37
Product	/38
Price	/37
Place	/28
Promoting by advertising	/35
Other types of promotion	/34

Exam hints

Planning
- Find out the **dates** of your Business Studies examination. Make an examination and revision **timetable**.

Revising
- Business Studies should be revised **actively**. You should be doing more than just reading.
- After completing a topic in **school**, go through the topic again in the **GCSE Business Studies Success Guide**. Copy out the **main points** into a notebook or use a **highlighter** to emphasise them.
- Try and write out the **key points** from memory. Check what you have written and see if there are any differences.
- Revise in short bursts of about **30 minutes**, followed by a **short break**.
- Learn **facts** from your exercise books, notebooks and the **Success Guide**.
- Do the **multiple-choice** and **quiz-style questions** in this book and check your solutions.
- Once you feel confident that you know the topic, do the **examination-style** questions in this book. Highlight the key words in the question, **plan** your answer and then go back and **check** that you have answered the question.
- **Make a note** of any topics that you do not understand and go back through the notes again.
- Use the **homework diary** to keep track of the topics you have covered and your **scores**.

Different types of questions
- **Short-answer questions:** these often require just a one-word answer, or you may be asked to select the right answer from several alternatives.
- **Recall and application questions:** these often use words such as 'list', 'state' and 'describe', where you show your knowledge of key business concepts, using the context given in the exam paper.
- **Analysis and evaluation questions:** these are more demanding questions that ask you to 'explain', 'analyse', 'discuss' and 'evaluate'. You are often expected to show both sides of a business argument or decision, and you may have to make a judgement.

Getting ready for the examination
- Read the instructions **carefully** and do what you are asked to do: questions that use words such as '**list**' or '**state**' expect less detailed answers than those using words such as '**explain**'.
- Use the business **examples** and **context** provided to help you answer the question: **always** be prepared to refer to the context in your answers.
- Remember the business **vocabulary** you have learned: use 'business' words such as '**profit**', '**loan**' and '**promotion**' correctly.
- Note the exam paper **layout**: the answer lines given are often an indication of **how much to write**.
- If you are asked to **calculate** or use figures, make sure you show **all workings:** you can still get marks for the correct method even if your final answer is wrong.
- Keep an eye on the **time** and complete the paper: allow enough time to **check** your answers, and if you finish early, check everything and fill in any **gaps**.
- Last but not least: **don't panic!** Follow the advice above and do your best.

Good luck!

Our economy

A

Choose just one answer: a, b, c or d.

1 ***Sainsbury* and *Tesco* are:**
a) directors
b) competitors
c) partners
d) owners (1 mark)

2 **'Division of labour' refers to:**
a) workers arguing
b) staff who vote for different political parties
c) people specialising in jobs at work
d) managers who divide their staff between themselves (1 mark)

3 **A business risk-taker is known as an:**
a) entrepreneur
b) expert
c) employee
d) enabler (1 mark)

4 **How a firm's activities affect the environment is explained by its:**
a) balance sheet
b) articles of association
c) ethical policies
d) HRM department (1 mark)

5 **Buying a new machine increases a firm's:**
a) land
b) labour
c) capital
d) enterprise (1 mark)

Score /5

B

Answer all parts of all questions.

1 **An arrow has been drawn from each factor of production to a reward. Correct any errors in these pairings.**

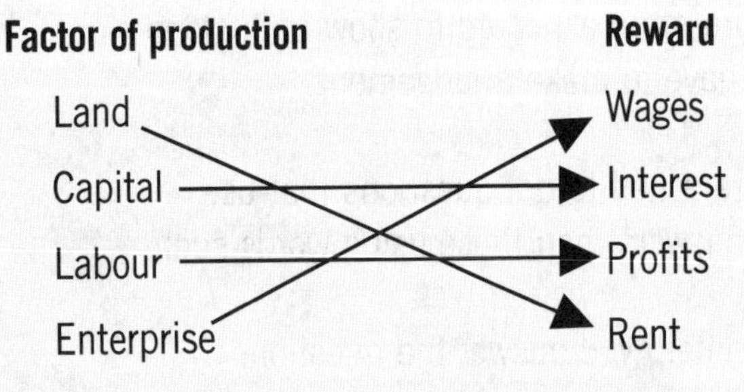

(4 marks)

2 **Match each factor of production below with the correct description and example.**

Factor	Description	Example
a) Land	i) Investment in major resources	1) Finance clerk
b) Labour	ii) Men and women available to work	2) Farming
c) Capital	iii) Risk-takers	3) Owner
d) Enterprise	iv) Raw materials and space	4) New machine

(8 marks)

Score /12

C

These are GCSE-style questions. Answer all parts of the questions. Continue on a separate sheet where necessary.

1 ***Daccord plc*** **is a large manufacturing business that makes electrical goods. It uses new technology, and its production is highly specialised.**

a) Explain two advantages to *Daccord plc* of using specialisation.

....

....

....

.... **(4 marks)**

b) Outline one disadvantage to *Daccord plc* of using specialisation.

....

.... **(2 marks)**

2 **Jane and John run a partnership selling fruit and vegetables. Their shop is busy, and they wish to expand.**

a) Name three examples of factors of production (resources) that would help their business expand.

....

.... **(3 marks)**

b) Explain two important influences on the level of demand for Jane and John's goods.

....

.... **(4 marks)**

c) Jane handles the financial side of the business, and John deals with marketing and staff recruitment. Explain why this arrangement is likely to benefit their business.

....

....

.... **(6 marks)**

Score /19

For more on this topic see pages 4–5 of your Success Guide.

Total score /36

How well did you do? ✗ 0–7 Try again 8–18 Getting there 19–29 Good work 29–36 Excellent! ✓

Types of economy

A

Choose just one answer: a, b, c or d.

1 A feature of the free market economy is that:
a) individuals and the state are in partnership
b) most companies are in the public sector
c) the state controls the economy's resources
d) prices are set through the price mechanism
(1 mark)

2 In a mixed economy:
a) all prices are set by the government
b) supply and demand are always the same
c) both public and private sectors are found
d) the public and private sectors must be the same size **(1 mark)**

3 In a planned economy, prices are set by:
a) directors
b) the state
c) customers
d) supply and demand **(1 mark)**

4 Where the demand for a product is greater than its supply, its price will normally:
a) fall
b) rise
c) stay the same
d) fall then rise **(1 mark)**

5 Where the demand for a product equals its supply, they are:
a) in excess
b) in equilibrium
c) entrepreneurial
d) economic **(1 mark)**

Score /5

B

Answer all parts of all questions.

1 Classify the following as either goods or services:

hairdresser	shampoo	towels	car	petrol	garage
....	....	....	....	....	....

(6 marks)

2 Complete the following sentences, using the correct word or phrase from the list underneath.

In a free market economy, entrepreneurs are encouraged by the ....

In a planned economy, the state decides .... is made, ... it is made, and .... it is made. A mixed economy contains both .... and .... sectors: these have objectives to make a .... and provide a .... respectively.

profit motive	product	supply	demand	public	personnel	who	how
price mechanism	what	profit	service	where	surplus	private	

(8 marks)

Score /14

C

These are GCSE-style questions. Answer all parts of the questions. Continue on a separate sheet where necessary.

1 Examples of business objectives – 'targets' set by the owner(s) of a business – include:

- **maximising profit**
- **survival**
- **increasing market share**

Explain, using examples where appropriate, what is meant by each of these terms:

Maximising profit: ....

....

Survival: ....

....

Increasing market share: ....

.... **(9 marks)**

2 *Inkright Ltd*, a company making inks for pens and printers, has a number of objectives. Choose an appropriate definition for the words underlined in each objective below.

Objective

i) To widen our <u>target market</u>. ....

ii) To improve our <u>brand loyalty</u>. ....

iii) To increase <u>employee productivity</u>. ....

iv) To control our <u>fixed costs</u>. ....

Definition

a) The amount of profit left after all costs have been deducted.
b) A fall in the price of goods.
c) An increase in the work done in a day by staff.
d) The expenses that must be paid regardless of output.
e) The people who might buy the product.
f) Expenses that are directly related to the products being made.
g) Customers who buy the same product again and again. **(4 marks)**

3 *KingPrawns* is a <u>private sector</u> firm that sells sandwiches and other lunchtime snacks to staff working in a <u>public sector</u> business. Explain the terms underlined here.

....

.... **(2 marks)**

Score /15

For more on this topic see pages 6–7 of your Success Guide.

Total score /34

How well did you do? ✗ 0–8 Try again 9–17 Getting there 18–26 Good work 27–34 Excellent! ✓

Locating business

A

Choose just one answer: a, b, c or d.

1 A business that makes children's toys is in the:
a) primary sector
b) secondary sector
c) tertiary sector
d) quarterly sector **(1 mark)**

2 A business that sells these toys is in the:
a) primary sector
b) secondary sector
c) tertiary sector
d) quarterly sector **(1 mark)**

3 An influence on the location of a new garage is the:
a) number of people who watch TV
b) change in demand for cars in the UK
c) level of fuel tax
d) competition in the area **(1 mark)**

4 When workers move to the work, this is called:
a) occupational mobility
b) operational mobility
c) historical mobility
d) geographical mobility **(1 mark)**

5 A primary sector business:
a) extracts something
b) constructs something
c) manufactures something
d) services something **(1 mark)**

Score /5

B

Answer all parts of all questions.

1 *GreatHols Ltd* sells holidays. Its head office is in London, and the directors are concerned about the high cost of rent being paid. There is also little room to expand, and staff find it difficult to travel to the head office.

From the list below, identify the three most important influences on where the head office might be relocated.

Influence
a) Low business rent and rates
b) Parking for staff
c) Parking for people buying holidays
d) Near an airport used by holidaymakers
e) Close to city-centre facilities (banks, restaurants, etc.)
f) Room to build an extension
g) In the country
h) Good road and rail connections

(3 marks)

2 *Buildright Ltd* constructs commercial buildings. Name three services in the tertiary sector that would support *Buildright Ltd.*

....

(3 marks)

Score /6

C

These are GCSE-style questions. Answer all parts of the questions. Continue on a separate sheet where necessary.

1 **Jane and John are in partnership, running a shop that sells fruit and vegetables. Their friend, Rob, grows produce that is sold in the shop.**

a) Name the sector of the economy in which the partnership is based.

.... **(1 mark)**

b) Name the sector that Rob works in.

.... **(1 mark)**

2 **One popular reason for a business staying where it is, rather than moving, is its existing workforce. Explain two reasons why this is often the case.**

....

.... **(4 marks)**

3 ***Elextrix Ltd* makes electrical components. The company is located in the port area of what used to be a large and thriving seaside town. Many local people work at the site. The port area has become run down, and the directors want to relocate the company. The local council is developing the old port into a residential and leisure area, and the directors know they can sell the company's premises for redevelopment.**

a) Explain two factors the directors will need to consider before they decide to relocate.

....

....

.... **(4 marks)**

b) Outline the problems the company may face if the decision to relocate to a new area is taken.

....

.... **(3 marks)**

c) Consider the possible effects of the proposed changes in the area on the local community.

....

....

.... **(4 marks)**

Score /17

For more on this topic see pages 8–9 of your Success Guide.

Total score /28

How well did you do? ✗ 0–6 Try again 7–14 Getting there 15–21 Good work 22–28 Excellent! ✓

The European Union

A

Choose just one answer: a, b, c or d.

1 The EU produces laws known as:
a) demarcations
b) decisions
c) directives
d) differentials (1 mark)

2 The UK's main market is:
a) the EU
b) the USA
c) Asia
d) Africa (1 mark)

3 The unit of currency used in most of the EU is the:
a) dollar b) euro
c) pound d) yen (1 mark)

4 The CE mark on a product indicates that it:
a) was 'Constructed in Europe'
b) is damaged, and is being sold at a loss
c) can be 'Changed in England'
d) meets health and safety requirements (1 mark)

5 The UK imports from other EU countries about:
a) 10% of its products
b) 25% of its products
c) 60% of its products
d) 99% of its products (1 mark)

Score /5

B

Answer all parts of all questions.

1 Label the following pie chart, which shows the UK's exports (2006).

The missing labels are:
North and South America
the EU
Asia and Oceania
the rest of the world

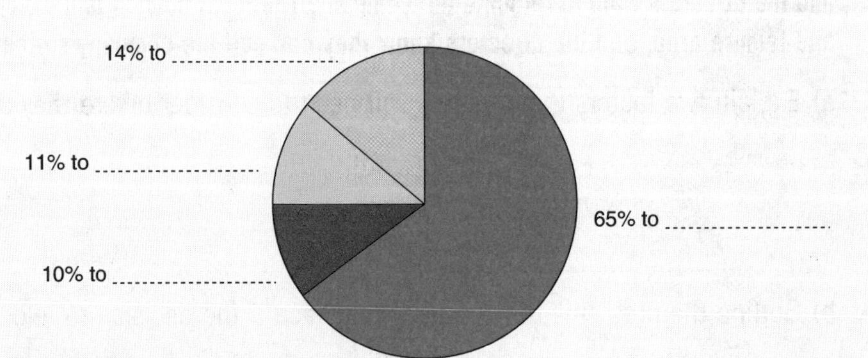

(4 marks)

2 Delete the incorrect word or phrase from each of the following sentences.

If the UK joins the Eurozone, exchange rate fluctuations will start taking place/will no longer take place. Price differences between countries will be easier to see/more difficult to see because all goods and services will be valued in euros/pounds.

(3 marks)

Score /7

C These are GCSE-style questions. Answer all parts of the questions. Continue on a separate sheet where necessary.

1 **Give two advantages and two disadvantages to UK businesses as a result of monetary union in most of the European Union.**

....

....

....

.... **(8 marks)**

2 ***Fitz Ltd* makes pens and pencils. These are currently sold in the UK only. The directors plan to start selling them in the rest of Europe. The directors have heard of the 'Single Market' but know little about it.**

a) i) Explain the main purposes of the EU's 'Single Market'.

....

....

.... **(4 marks)**

ii) Give three examples of the work of the 'Single Market'.

....

....

.... **(3 marks)**

b) Outline two other ways in which the European Union influences the work of UK firms.

....

.... **(4 marks)**

c) Suggest three problems that *Fitz Ltd* is likely to face when carrying out its plans to export to the rest of Europe.

....

....

.... **(6 marks)**

Score /25

For more on this topic see pages 10–11 of your Success Guide.

Total score /37

How well did you do? ✗ 0–7 Try again 8–17 Getting there 18–28 Good work 29–37 Excellent! ✓

International business

A

Choose just one answer: a, b, c or d.

1 The balance of trade measures the UK's:
a) visible trade
b) invisible trade
c) trade in services
d) trade in buying and selling assets **(1 mark)**

2 Selling goods abroad is called:
a) importing b) exporting
c) franchising d) specialising **(1 mark)**

3 A possible benefit of trading overseas is:
a) economies of scale
b) diseconomies of scale
c) greater competition
d) exchange rate fluctuations **(1 mark)**

4 One reason for the UK to trade with other countries is that:
a) it is easier than trading at home
b) trade barriers can be set up
c) it is the law to do so
d) not all raw materials exist here **(1 mark)**

5 An example of a trade barrier is a:
a) quota
b) quartile
c) questionnaire
d) quorum **(1 mark)**

Score /5

B

Answer all parts of all questions.

1 Match each trade barrier with the correct alternative name and description.

Barrier	Alternative name	Description
a) Tariff	i) Import duty	1) The number of goods allowed into the country is limited
b) Quota	ii) Physical restriction	2) The price is raised to make the imported item less competitive

(4 marks)

2 Tick the relevant box to classify these as benefits to UK firms as a result of exporting, or benefits to UK firms as a result of importing.

	Exporting	Importing
a) The firm's sales will increase	☐	☐
b) The firm spreads risk by selling in different markets	☐	☐
c) There is greater choice	☐	☐
d) Supplies from abroad may be cheaper	☐	☐
e) The overseas market may be less saturated	☐	☐

(5 marks)

Score /9

C This is a GCSE-style question. Answer all parts of the question. Continue on a separate sheet where necessary.

1 ***Pushkids Ltd* makes children's pushchairs. These are sold in the UK. The directors want to start selling the pushchairs in overseas markets. Two directors wish to market the pushchairs in two EU countries – one wants to sell them in Ireland, and another would like to sell them in France. A third director wishes to export to the USA. To start with, the directors want to start exporting to one country only.**

a) Explain one possible benefit to *Pushkids Ltd*, and one likely benefit to its UK customers, as a result of the company deciding to export its products.

....

.... **(4 marks)**

b) Outline the main problems the directors of *Pushkids Ltd* are likely to face when planning to export the pushchairs to any overseas destination.

....

....

.... **(6 marks)**

c) Select one country to which the directors should choose to export the pushchairs. Justify your selection by reference to all three countries.

....

....

....

....

....

....

....

....

.... **(12 marks)**

Score /22

For more on this topic see pages 12–13 of your Success Guide.

Total score /36

How well did you do? 0–7 Try again 8–16 Getting there 17–27 Good work 28–36 Excellent!

Sole trader and partnership businesses

A

Choose just one answer: a, b, c or d.

1 One person owning a business is called a:
a) stakeholder
b) director
c) partner
d) sole trader (1 mark)

2 The liability of sole traders and partnerships is:
a) limited
b) unlimited
c) legal
d) partial (1 mark)

3 A sole trader:
a) can employ others
b) pays Corporation (company) Tax
c) has a separate legal existence from the business
d) has to share the business's profits (1 mark)

4 A partner putting money only into the business is:
a) an active partner
b) a specialist partner
c) a joint partner
d) a sleeping partner (1 mark)

5 Compared with a sole trader business:
a) partners can specialise
b) a partnership is easier to create
c) all partners have limited liability
d) partners find it harder to raise capital (1 mark)

Score /5

B

Answer all parts of all questions.

1 Delete the incorrect word or phrase in the following.

Three features of a partnership, compared with a sole trader, are:
i) the owners normally find it easier/harder to raise capital
ii) a partnership is easier/harder to set up
iii) partners can/cannot specialise. (3 marks)

2 Tick the appropriate box to identify these as features of either a sole trader, a partnership, or both.

	Sole trader	Partnership	Both
a) All the responsibility is held by one person	☐	☐	☐
b) Unlimited liability	☐	☐	☐
c) No need to share profits	☐	☐	☐
d) An agreement is usually drawn up	☐	☐	☐
e) More capital can be invested	☐	☐	☐
f) Quick decisions can be made	☐	☐	☐

(6 marks)

Score /9

C

This is a GCSE-style question. Answer all parts of the question. Continue on a separate sheet where necessary.

1 **Beverley runs her own hairdressing business as a sole trader. She has recently lost customers, and has found it difficult to pay her business bills.**

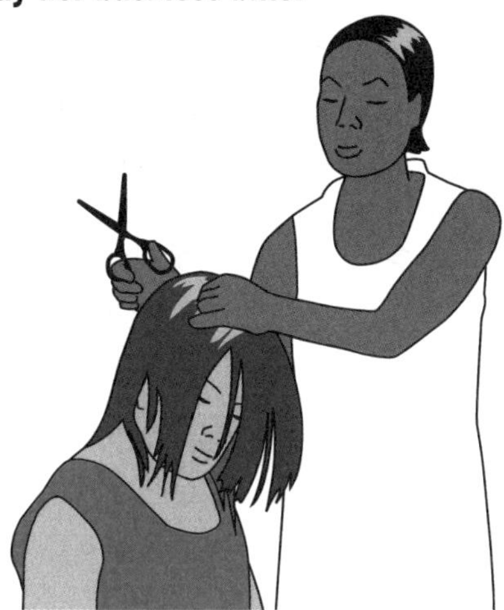

a) Describe how being an unincorporated business will affect Beverley if she cannot meet her business debts.

....

....

.... **(3 marks)**

Beverley is thinking of going into partnership with her friend, Rashid, who has experience in the field of marketing and advertising. Beverley believes that going into partnership will help her business prosper.

b) i) Explain two advantages to Beverley of going into partnership with Rashid.

....

....

.... **(4 marks)**

ii) Explain two disadvantages that Beverley will face as a result of this business decision.

....

....

.... **(4 marks)**

c) Outline how turning the business into a limited partnership might help Beverley and Rashid.

....

.... **(2 marks)**

d) Beverley and Rashid have decided to go into partnership. Identify three likely items that they will include in their partnership agreement.

....

.... **(3 marks)**

Score /16

For more on this topic see pages 14–15 of your Success Guide. Total score /30

How well did you do? ✗ 0–6 Try again 7–15 Getting there 16–24 Good work 25–30 Excellent! ✓

Limited companies

A

Choose just one answer: a, b, c or d.

1 Each year, a limited company has to prepare:
a) an invoice b) a statement
c) an article d) an annual report
(1 mark)

2 A public limited company, but not a private limited company:
a) issues dividends to its shareholders
b) pays taxes to the government
c) produces accounts for its shareholders
d) trades its shares on the Stock Exchange
(1 mark)

3 Limited liability:
a) encourages people to invest
b) allows companies to keep their affairs private
c) only applies to public limited companies
d) stops takeover bids (1 mark)

4 The memorandum of association explains a company's:
a) financial accounts
b) business documents
c) internal relationships
d) external relationships (1 mark)

5 'Separation of ownership from control' refers to:
a) shareholders and owners
b) shareholders and directors
c) directors and staff
d) staff and shareholders (1 mark)

Score /5

B

Answer all parts of all questions.

1 Study these business features. Identify them as relevant to a sole trader, a partnership or a public limited company by ticking the relevant box.

	Sole trader	Partnership	Limited company
a) Owner's death does not end the business	☐	☐	☐
b) It has between 2 and 20 owners	☐	☐	☐
c) It has limited liability	☐	☐	☐
d) Owner finds it difficult to take time off	☐	☐	☐
e) Shares can be bought by the public	☐	☐	☐
f) One person owns the firm	☐	☐	☐

(6 marks)

2 Delete the incorrect word or phrase in the following sentences.

Compared with plcs, a private limited company is more likely/less likely to suffer from 'red tape' because it is normally much smaller/bigger. The shares of a private company can/cannot be traded on the Stock Exchange. As a result, it is more likely/less likely to be the subject of a hostile takeover bid.
(4 marks)

C

These are GCSE-style questions. Answer all parts of the questions. Continue on a separate sheet where necessary.

1 ***Waterworks plc*** **manufactures drinks that it sells to major retailers such as** ***Sainsbury's*** **and** ***Tesco.*** **Below are some business terms that could apply to** ***Waterworks plc.***

Limited liability	**Sole traders**	**Primary sector**
Secondary sector	**Baltic Exchange**	**Stock Exchange**
Mass production	**Job production**	**Shareholders**
Unlimited liability	**Partners**	**Tertiary sector**

Select the terms that best answer the following questions.

a) What is the name for the owners of *Waterworks plc*? ....

b) What liability do these owners have? ....

c) In which sector of the economy does *Waterworks plc* operate? ....

d) What type of production does *Waterworks plc* use? ....

e) Where can shares of *Waterworks plc* be traded? .... **(5 marks)**

2 **Eric has shares in** ***Tesco*****, and is a director of a small company. Explain how Eric's role as a shareholder is different from his role as a director.**

....

....

....

.... **(8 marks)**

3 **Horel and Lardy are in partnership. They are now thinking of converting their partnership into a private limited company. Explain three reasons why they might decide to do so.**

....

....

.... **(6 marks)**

Score /19

For more on this topic see pages 16–17 of your Success Guide.

Total score /34

How well did you do? ✗ 0–8 Try again 9–17 Getting there 18–26 Good work 27–34 Excellent! ✓

Other businesses

A

Choose just one answer: a, b, c or d.

1 In the UK, a multinational business is normally:
a) a sole trader
b) a partnership
c) a private limited company
d) a public limited company (1 mark)

2 A franchisor is:
a) the person who takes out a franchise
b) the company granting the franchise
c) the person who buys the product
d) a supplier to the franchise company (1 mark)

3 Public corporations are owned by:
a) shareholders b) directors
c) the state d) executives (1 mark)

4 A disadvantage to the UK from having multinational businesses is that they:
a) export their profits
b) provide work opportunities
c) bring in new ideas
d) help keep the economy competitive (1 mark)

5 'CWS' stands for:
a) Co-operative Wholesale Society
b) Co-operative Women's Society
c) Co-operative Welfare Society
d) Co-operative Workers' Society (1 mark)

Score /5

B

Answer all parts of all questions.

1 Delete the incorrect word or phrase from the following sentences.

The company that awards a franchise is called the franchisor/franchisee, and the person who takes on this franchise is known as a franchisor/franchisee. The franchising company supplies the product/customers and capital/expertise, and in return receives a product/capital. (4 marks)

2 Are the following statements about multinational companies found in the UK economy true or false?

	True	False
a) They may bring in new expertise	☐	☐
b) They can influence the government's policies	☐	☐
c) They operate in the form of partnerships	☐	☐
d) They sometimes export their profits	☐	☐
e) They employ only foreign labour	☐	☐
f) They never pay any taxes in the UK	☐	☐

(6 marks)

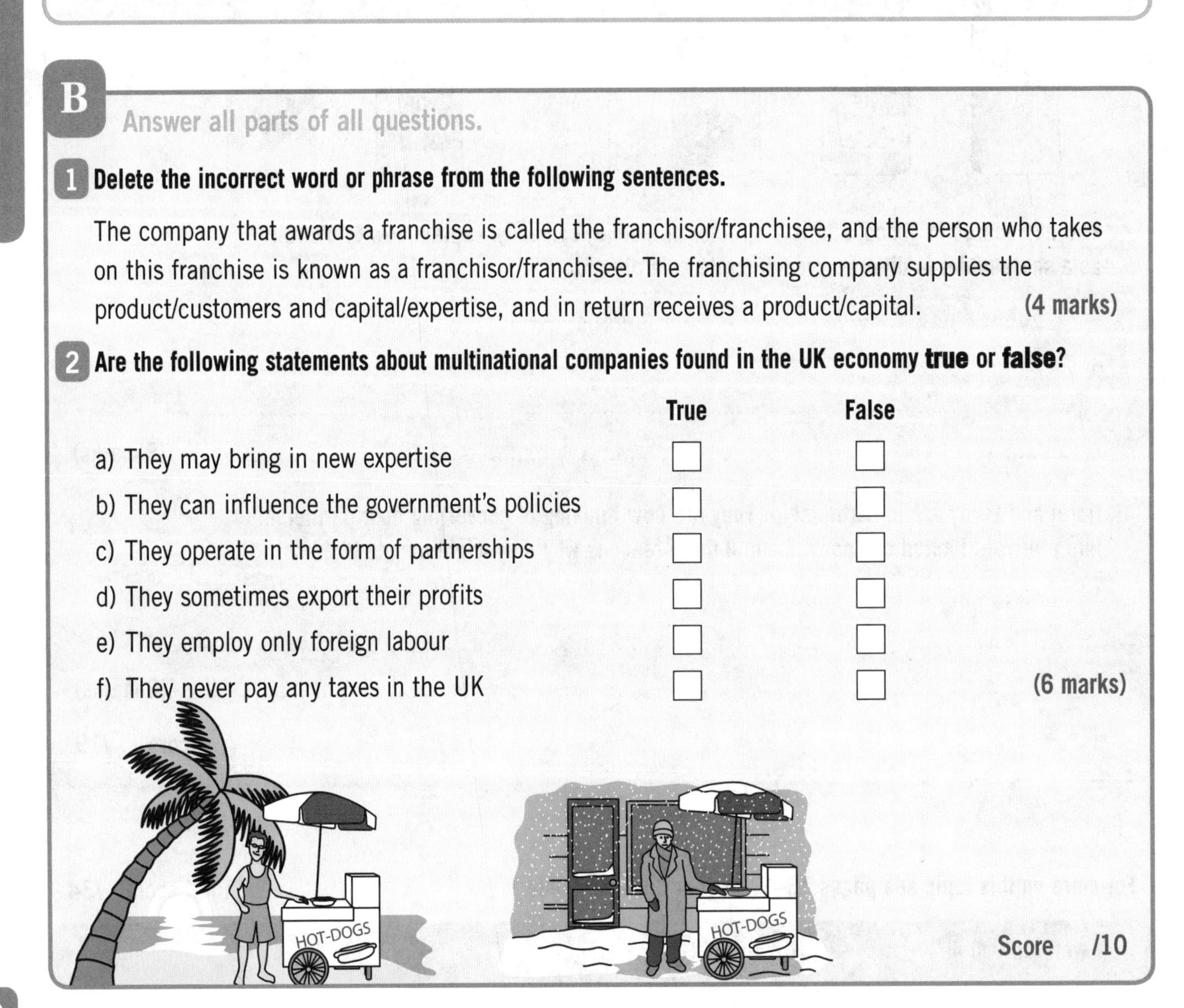

Score /10

C

These are GCSE-style questions. Answer all parts of the questions. Continue on a separate sheet where necessary.

1 Vincent has read an advertisement placed by *Dave's DVDs*, offering franchises in renting DVDs to the public.

a) Advise Vincent of the advantages and disadvantages associated with taking on a franchise.

....

.... (4 marks)

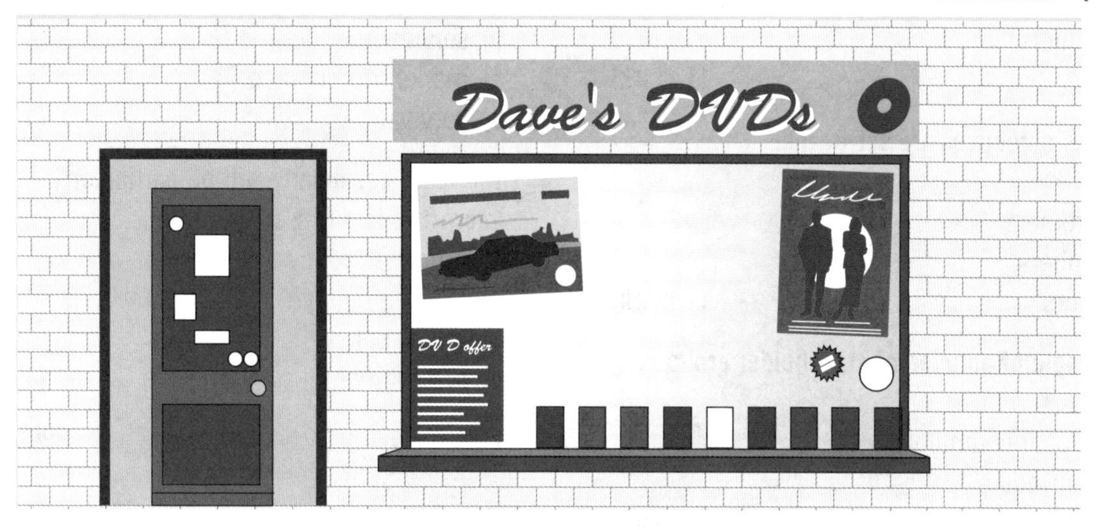

b) Give two reasons why businesses such as *Dave's DVDs* prefer to grow through offering franchises rather than by opening their own new branches.

....

.... (4 marks)

2 Dyanne works for a multinational company that has factories in Wales. She has recently ended her employment with a public corporation.

a) Define the terms 'multinational company' and 'public corporation'.

....

.... (2 marks)

b) Suggest two advantages and two disadvantages to the UK economy of having multinational companies operating in its economy.

....

.... (4 marks)

c) Explain, using examples, two advantages of keeping some firms or industries in public ownership.

....

.... (4 marks)

Score /18

For more on this topic see pages 18–19 of your Success Guide.

Total score /33

How well did you do? ✗ 0–6 Try again 7–16 Getting there 17–26 Good work 27–33 Excellent! ✓

Stakeholders in business

A

Choose just one answer: a, b, c or d.

1 Customers are an example of a firm's:
a) shareholders
b) stakeholders
c) suppliers
d) staff (1 mark)

2 Business objectives are set by the:
a) staff
b) customers
c) suppliers
d) owners (1 mark)

3 An example of an internal stakeholder group is:
a) lenders
b) the local community
c) employees
d) suppliers (1 mark)

4 Public sector organisations typically have objectives based on:
a) profits
b) service
c) market dominance
d) survival (1 mark)

5 The local community will be particularly interested in a firm's:
a) financial policy
b) lending policy
c) credit policy
d) environmental policy (1 mark)

Score /5

B

Answer all parts of all questions.

1 Match each business objective to the correct description.

Objective	Description
a) Growth	i) Diversifying into different products and/or markets
b) Market share	ii) Trying to stay in business, even if making a loss
c) Survival	iii) Setting a target for net income from the business
d) Profit	iv) Trying to get a larger percentage of the total sales

(4 marks)

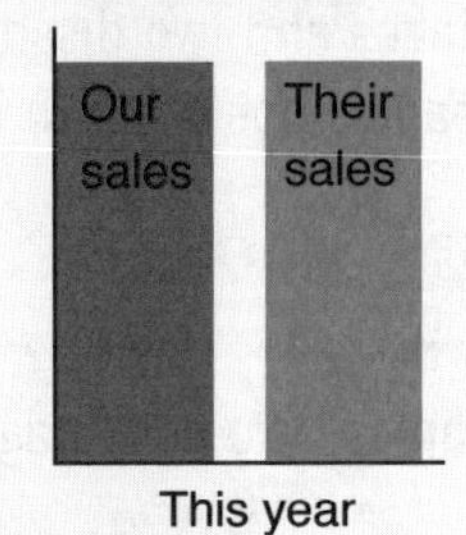

2 Match an appropriate aim to each stakeholder group.

Group	Aim
a) Customers	i) No pollution in the surrounding area
b) Local community	ii) A return on their investment in the firm
c) Lenders	iii) Job security
d) Employees	iv) Lower prices

(4 marks)

Score /8

C

This is a GCSE-style question. Answer all parts of the question. Continue on a separate sheet where necessary.

1 ***Eatwell Ltd*** **is a large farming business in England. Its main business aim is 'growth through diversification'. The company owns a number of farms, and employs over 20 people. There is also a 'farm park' for children, where families are invited to meet young animals, and a craft centre on nearby land owned by** ***Eatwell Ltd.*** **In this centre, a number of sole traders rent outlets from** ***Eatwell Ltd*** **and make products that they sell to people visiting the farm park.**

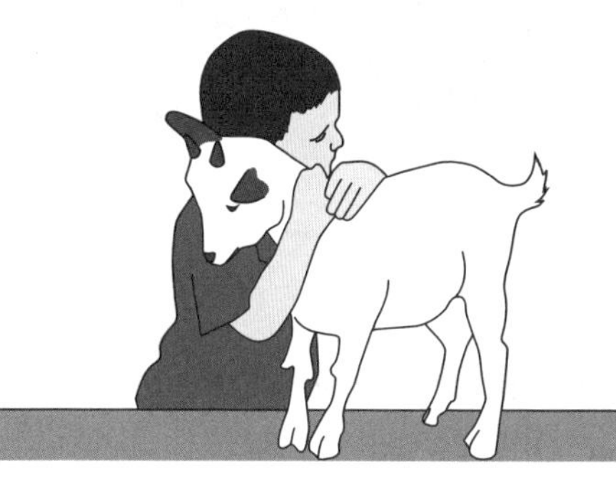

Eatwell Ltd **has links with a number of businesses, including** ***Growlots plc*****, a large farming equipment manufacturer, and** ***DEFRA*****, the government department that deals with agriculture and rural matters.**

a) i) Explain what the main aim of *Eatwell Ltd* means.

....

.... **(2 marks)**

ii) From the above information, state two examples that suggest *Eatwell Ltd* is carrying out this business aim.

....

.... **(2 marks)**

iii) Suggest two advantages to *Eatwell Ltd* if the company manages to achieve this business aim.

....

.... **(4 marks)**

b) Assess how relevant the same business aim is likely to be for the following organisations:

i) *Lee Arthurs*, a sole trader in the craft centre, who sells paintings and artists' materials.

....

....

.... **(4 marks)**

ii) *Growlots plc*, the farming equipment manufacturer.

....

....

.... **(4 marks)**

iii) *DEFRA*, the government department.

....

....

.... **(4 marks)**

Score /20

For more on this topic see pages 20–21 of your Success Guide.

Total score /33

How well did you do? ✗ 0–6 Try again | 7–15 Getting there | 16–25 Good work | 26–33 Excellent! ✓

The main functions of business

A

Choose just one answer: a, b, c or d.

1 'Personnel' is another name for the:
a) Finance department
b) Human Resource Management department
c) Marketing department
d) Production department **(1 mark)**

2 An example of work that is not a finance activity is:
a) paying bills
b) arranging loans
c) calculating profit or loss
d) appointing staff **(1 mark)**

3 Studying the product lifecycle is carried out in:
a) Marketing b) Finance
c) Production d) Personnel **(1 mark)**

4 Functions of the HRM Department include:
a) setting up lean production methods
b) buying sales representatives' new cars
c) setting a price for the firm's product
d) negotiating with trade unions **(1 mark)**

5 'Promotion' in the Marketing Department involves:
a) re-grading staff
b) distributing the products
c) advertising the products
d) market research **(1 mark)**

Score /5

B

Answer all parts of all questions.

1 Underline any of the following functions that are typical of a marketing department.

Recruiting new staff
Looking after the staff
Arranging loans
Research and development
Planning production runs
Carrying out market research
Buying raw materials
Advertising products
Paying staff

(2 marks)

2 Match each marketing term with its example.

Term	Example
a) Product	i) Following a 'skimming' strategy
b) Price	ii) Using a wholesaler
c) Place	iii) Carrying out direct marketing
d) Promotion	iv) Studying market segmentation

(4 marks)

Score /6

C

These are GCSE-style questions. Answer all parts of the questions. Continue on a separate sheet where necessary.

1 **Study the organisation chart for *Nicetaste Ltd*, shown on page 27.**
Describe the work carried out in these departments of *Nicetaste Ltd*:

a) the Finance department: ....

....

b) the Marketing department: ....

....

c) the Production department: ....

.... **(6 marks)**

2 ***Buildit Ltd* is a construction company that builds houses. The company's Human Resource Management (HRM) department is based at its head office in Liverpool, where some staff training is carried out. *Buildit Ltd* also uses local colleges as training providers.**

a) List four other functions you would expect this company's HRM Department to carry out.

....

.... **(4 marks)**

b) The company offers induction training, on-the-job training, and off-the-job training.

i) Distinguish between these three forms of training.

....

....

.... **(6 marks)**

ii) Name the type of training that is most likely to be carried out in the local colleges.

.... **(1 mark)**

c) *Buildit Ltd* uses job production methods for individually designed houses, and batch production methods for houses of an identical design. Explain the difference between these two forms of production.

....

.... **(4 marks)**

Score /21

For more on this topic see pages 24–25 of your Success Guide.

Total score /32

How well did you do? ✗ 0–6 Try again 7–14 Getting there 15–24 Good work 25–32 Excellent! ✓

Organising business

A

Choose just one answer: a, b, c or d.

1 Managers who ask other staff to do work on their behalf are:
a) depreciating
b) delayering
c) delegating
d) deflating **(1 mark)**

2 The chain of command in a business is shown by its:
a) span of control
b) organisation chart
c) production budget
d) current liabilities **(1 mark)**

3 'Hierarchy' refers to a firm's:
a) organisation
b) products
c) services
d) equipment **(1 mark)**

4 A tall organisation structure is associated with:
a) short chains of command
b) wide spans of control
c) specialised staff
d) fast decision-making **(1 mark)**

5 A matrix structure is when the firm is organised:
a) externally
b) by role
c) by department
d) by task **(1 mark)**

Score /5

B

Answer all parts of the question.

1 ***Sportsware plc*** **is a large company that sells sports clothing. The company is controlled by the board of directors, which appoints a managing director. There are four departments – Purchasing, Sales, Accounts and Human Resources – and each one has a departmental manager.**

a) Using this information, complete the organisation chart below.

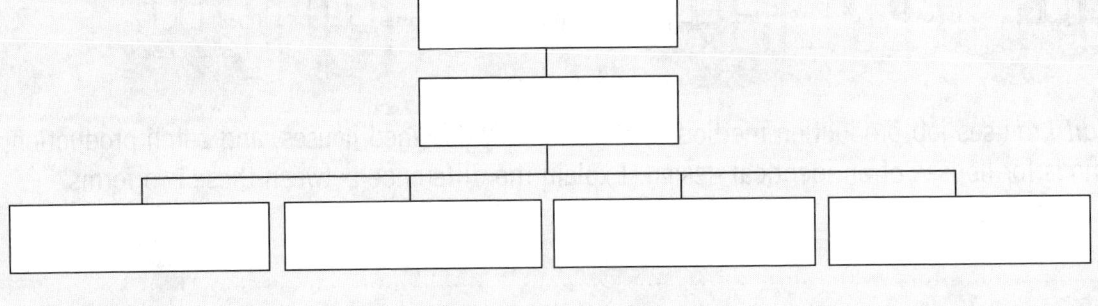

(3 marks)

b) Match each department with an example of its main work.

Department	Example of work
i) Purchasing	1) Carrying out staff appraisals
ii) Accounts	2) Visiting potential customers
iii) Sales	3) Arranging deliveries of clothing to be sold later
iv) Human Resources	4) Arranging finance for a new display stand

(4 marks)

Score /7

C

This is a GCSE-style question. Answer all parts of the question. Continue on a separate sheet where necessary.

1 **The organisation chart below is for *Nicetaste Ltd*, a food manufacturer that sells its products to small and medium-sized grocery businesses in the UK.**

- **Board of Directors**
  - **Managing Director**
    - **HR Director**
      - **Staff Welfare Manager** – **4 staff**
      - **Recruitment Manager** – **2 staff**
    - **Finance Director**
      - **Accounts Manager** – **5 staff**
    - **Marketing Director**
      - **Sales Manager** – **8 staff**
    - **Production Director**
      - **Production Manager** – **6 staff**
      - **Chief Buyer** – **2 staff**

a) Explain the terms:

i) Span of control ....

ii) Chain of command ....

iii) Hierarchy .... **(6 marks)**

b) State the span of control of the Finance Director: .... **(1 mark)**

c) To whom will the Chief Buyer report if there is a problem? .... **(1 mark)**

d) Give two reasons why an organisation chart such as this is helpful to a business.

....

.... **(4 marks)**

e) Using examples from the organisation chart, explain the terms 'authority', 'responsibility' and 'accountability'.

....

....

....

.... **(6 marks)**

Score /18

For more on this topic see pages 26–27 of your Success Guide.

Total score /30

How well did you do? ✗ 0–6 Try again 7–14 Getting there 15–23 Good work 24–30 Excellent! ✓

Communicating in business

A

Choose just one answer: a, b, c or d.

1 Meetings and using the telephone are examples of:
a) oral communication
b) written communication
c) electronic communication
d) poor communication (1 mark)

2 The sender of a message is called the:
a) transferor
b) transaction
c) translator
d) transmitter (1 mark)

3 An example of a visual communication method is a:
a) bar chart
b) letter
c) price list
d) quotation (1 mark)

4 'Minutes' of a meeting state:
a) what the meeting will be about
b) where the meeting is to take place
c) how long the meeting is expected to last
d) what was said at the meeting (1 mark)

5 A statement of account is a:
a) production report
b) summary of overheads
c) trading document
d) list of staff (1 mark)

Score /5

B

Answer all parts of all questions.

1 Place these trading documents into their correct order, indicating whether they flow from buyer to seller, or from seller to buyer. The first one has been completed for you.

Document	Correct order	From:
a) Invoice		buyer to seller/seller to buyer
b) Advice note		buyer to seller/seller to buyer
c) Order		buyer to seller/seller to buyer
d) Payment		buyer to seller/seller to buyer
e) Letter of enquiry	1	buyer to seller/~~seller to buyer~~
f) Quotation		buyer to seller/seller to buyer
g) Statement of account		buyer to seller/seller to buyer
h) Delivery note		buyer to seller/seller to buyer

(7 marks)

2 Identify from the following list the items that will not appear on an invoice.

Address of buyer
Previous payments made
Amount of profit
Details of VAT
Total amount payable
Details of income tax
Address of seller
Cheque number
Last month's amount owed

ENQUIRIES QUOTATIONS

(5 marks)

Score /12

C **These are GCSE-style questions. Answer all parts of the questions. Continue on a separate sheet where necessary.**

1 **Jackie is a sole trader. She does all her own administration, but has to employ an accountant to 'do the books'. Jackie and the accountant meet every three months. Each year the accountant produces Jackie's Profit and Loss Account and her Balance Sheet, and then meets with Jackie.**

Explain why a meeting is an appropriate form of communication:

a) for the quarterly business between Jackie and her accountant.

....

.... (4 marks)

b) every year after the final accounts have been prepared.

....

.... (4 marks)

2 ***Tasco plc*** **is a major retailer, having branches throughout the UK. The company's head office is in London, and staff in the head office often communicate with branches by memo, telephone and e-mail. The company publishes its 'in-house' magazine each quarter.**

a) Describe why the staff use memos rather than letters to communicate with each other.

.... (2 marks)

b) The head office of *Tasco plc* urgently needs sales figures from its Wolverhampton branch. Compare e-mail and telephone as methods to communicate this information.

....

....

....

....

.... (8 marks)

c) Give two benefits to staff at *Tasco plc* from receiving a company magazine on a regular basis.

....

.... (4 marks)

Score /22

For more on this topic see pages 28–29 of your Success Guide.

Total score /39

How well did you do? ✗ 0–8 Try again 9–19 Getting there 20–30 Good work 31–39 Excellent! ✓

How a business grows

A

Choose just one answer: a, b, c or d.

1 When two businesses agree to join together, this is known as a:

a) takeover b) takeaway
c) merger d) mortgage (1 mark)

2 When firms in different industries join together, this is called:

a) vertical integration
b) horizontal integration
c) lateral integration
d) diagonal integration (1 mark)

3 One measure of a firm's size is to check the number of staff:

a) employed b) sacked
c) trained d) recruited (1 mark)

4 Firms that grow internally are said to grow:

a) locally
b) horizontally
c) organically
d) industrially (1 mark)

5 For a takeover to take place, one firm must buy the other firm's:

a) assets
b) liabilities
c) voting shares
d) staff (1 mark)

Score /5

B

Answer all parts of all questions.

1 Match the method of growth with its correct description.

Method	**Firms that:**
a) Organic	i) are in the same industry but at different stages of production
b) Horizontal	ii) are in different industries
c) Vertical	iii) are in the same industry and at the same stage of production
d) Lateral	iv) grow through internal expansion

(4 marks)

2 Identify the method of growth illustrated by each of these examples.

a) *Tesco*, the retailer, starts offering new products for sale. ....

b) *Texaco*, an oil company, buys an oilfield in Alaska. ....

c) The banks *TSB* and *Lloyds* join together. ....

d) A tobacco company buys a food manufacturer. ....

e) The car maker, *Toyota*, enters a new market. ....

f) *Morrisons*, a retailer, takes over another retailer. .... (6 marks)

Score /10

C

This is a GCSE-style question. Answer all parts of the question. Continue on a separate sheet where necessary.

1 **Mark and Tina own and run a small hotel in Blackpool. They have sunk all their savings into this business, and at present have no spare capital available. Mark and Tina cater for holidaymakers, and not business visitors, to Blackpool. At present they promote their business only through holiday brochures and magazines.**

Mark and Tina are proud of the personal service and attention they give to all visitors, and they have a very good reputation in the local area for the services they offer. They have plenty of space in the hotel, including several rooms that they use for storing surplus items.

a) Mark and Tina are pleased with the success of their business, and wish to expand. Describe two ways that they might expand their business internally.

....

.... **(4 marks)**

b) Explain why Mark and Tina might face difficulty expanding their business at the moment.

....

.... **(3 marks)**

c) Explain, using appropriate examples for Mark and Tina's business, how increasing in size might make them:

i) more successful

....

.... **(4 marks)**

ii) less successful.

....

.... **(4 marks)**

d) Mark and Tina have now expanded their business. Outline four ways by which they could measure how much their business has grown in a year's time.

....

.... **(4 marks)**

Score /19

For more on this topic see pages 30–31 of your Success Guide.

Total score /34

How well did you do? 0–6 Try again 7–16 Getting there 17–26 Good work 27–34 Excellent!

Supporting business

A

Choose just one answer: a, b, c or d.

1 'ONS' refers to the:
a) Office of Navy Ships
b) Organisation of Neighbourhood Shops
c) Office for National Statistics
d) Organisation for National Savings (1 mark)

2 The website address for government sites normally includes:
a) gov.uk
b) co.uk
c) com
d) ac.uk (1 mark)

3 UK Trade and Investment mainly supports:
a) UK exporters
b) overseas exporters
c) overseas workers
d) UK workers (1 mark)

4 An example of an ONS publication is:
a) Regional Trends
b) Fashion Trends
c) Taxation Trends
d) Government Trends (1 mark)

5 The Regional Development Fund is an example of:
a) UK publications
b) UK legislation
c) EU directives
d) EU financial support (1 mark)

Score /5

B

Answer all parts of the question.

1 Complete the following diagram, which shows typical areas of support for UK businesses.

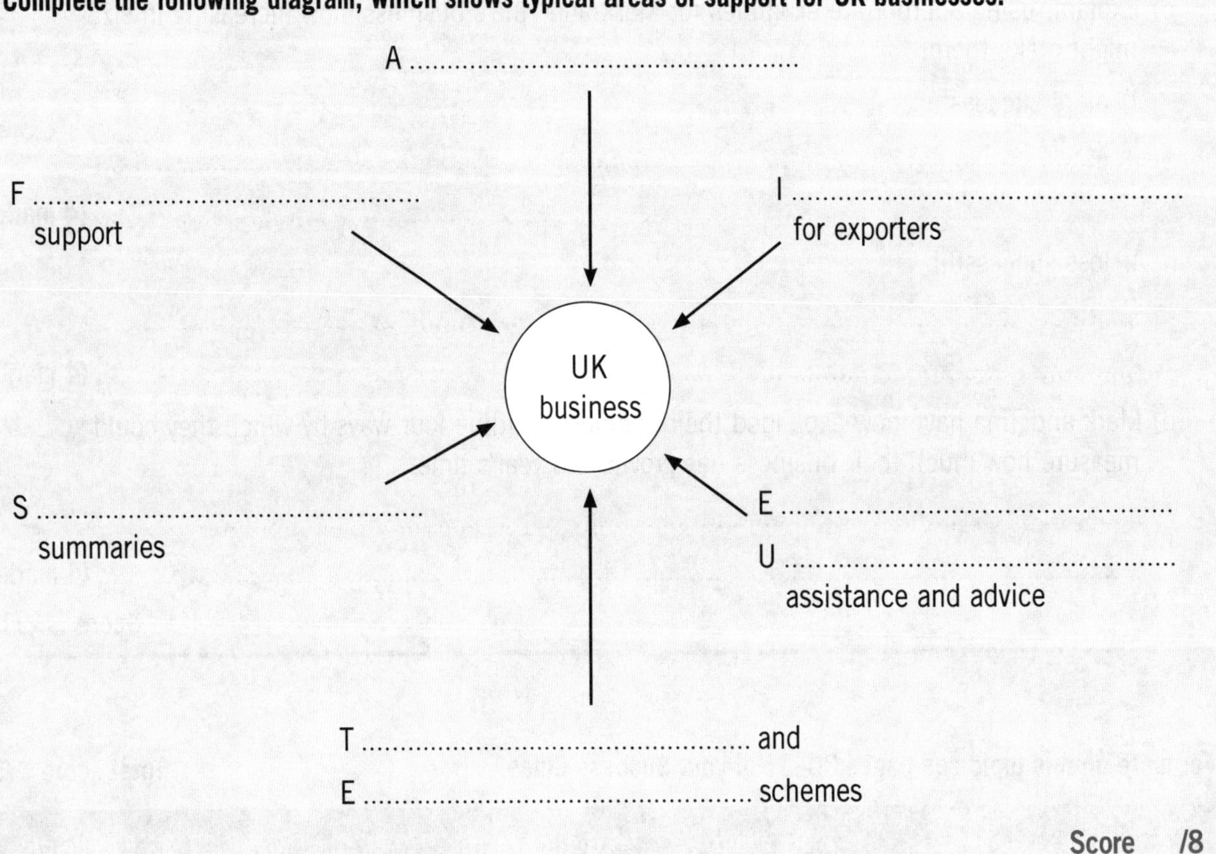

Score /8

C

These are GCSE-style questions. Answer all parts of the questions. Continue on a separate sheet where necessary.

1 **Explain the role of the following agencies:**

a) The Office for National Statistics (ONS) ....

....

b) UK Trade and Investment ....

....

c) The Export Credit Guarantee Department (ECGD). ....

.... **(6 marks)**

2 **Identify two reasons for UK businesses to be supported by the UK government.**

....

.... **(2 marks)**

3 **Explain why the European Union's Single Market can be considered as providing assistance to UK businesses.**

....

.... **(4 marks)**

4 **Jim Bentley makes specialist items of fitness equipment. He plans to expand his business, which will mean employing more staff and possibly moving to a different area.**

a) Outline ways in which the UK government might support Jim's decision to expand.

....

.... **(4 marks)**

b) Suggest two ways in which the European Union might support Jim if he decides to export his products to the rest of the EU.

....

.... **(4 marks)**

Score /20

For more on this topic see pages 32–33 of your Success Guide.

Total score /33

How well did you do? ✗ 0–6 Try again 7–16 Getting there 17–25 Good work 26–33 Excellent! ✓

Business and the law

A

Choose just one answer: a, b, c or d.

1 Health and safety laws are set by the:
a) company
b) Board of Directors
c) employees
d) government **(1 mark)**

2 Staff making products are protected by the:
a) Trade Descriptions Act
b) Health and Safety at Work Act
c) Sale of Goods Act
d) Road Traffic Act **(1 mark)**

3 All staff are covered in the workplace by:
a) delegation
b) legislation
c) equilibrium
d) communication **(1 mark)**

4 An example of consumer protection legislation is the:
a) Equal Pay Act
b) Trade Descriptions Act
c) Sex Discrimination Act
d) Part-time Work Directive **(1 mark)**

5 The Office of Fair Trading examines a firm's:
a) employment policies
b) assets and liabilities
c) trading activities
d) health and safety practices **(1 mark)**

Score /5

B

Answer all parts of all questions.

1 Match each act with the correct description.

Act	Description
a) Sale and Supply of Goods	i) Women and men who do the same work should receive the same reward
b) Trade Descriptions	ii) A firm should not treat a person who has a handicap differently from others
c) Disability Discrimination	iii) Employers and staff must take reasonable care of themselves and others
d) Race Relations	iv) Items sold must be of satisfactory quality and must be fit for their intended purpose
e) Equal Pay	v) There must be no discrimination on grounds such as nationality and ethnic origin
f) Health and Safety at Work	vi) It is a crime to describe goods incorrectly

(6 marks)

2 True or false? Under European Union legislation:

	True	False
a) everyone must be given a job	☐	☐
b) part-time staff should receive the same rights as full-time staff	☐	☐
c) the working week is limited to a maximum of 168 hours	☐	☐
d) employees can have (unpaid) leave when their child is born	☐	☐

(4 marks)

Score /10

C

These are GCSE-style questions. Answer all parts of the questions. Continue on a separate sheet where necessary.

1 **Name and describe three examples of EU directives.**

....

....

.... **(6 marks)**

2 **Identify and explain the effect of relevant laws in the following situations.**

a) Rachel has bought a sweatshirt from a high street store. She has just washed the sweatshirt for the first time, only to discover that it has shrunk and no longer fits her.

Name of relevant law: ....

Effect: ....

.... **(3 marks)**

b) David has bought a micro hi-fi unit from a specialist shop. The unit is in a box, and is described as having a 'brown casing'. When David opens the box, he sees that the casing is in fact grey.

Name of relevant law: ....

Effect: ....

.... **(3 marks)**

c) Stu Pid and Harry Sponsible are 'fooling around' at work. Stu injures Harry by throwing a hammer at him.

Name of relevant law: ....

Effect: ....

.... **(3 marks)**

d) Jayne and John both joined their company at the same time and do the same job. John is paid £5.50 an hour, and Jayne is paid £5.25 an hour.

Name of relevant law: ....

Effect: ....

.... **(3 marks)**

Score /18

For more on this topic see pages 34–35 of your Success Guide.

Total score /33

How well did you do? ✗ 0–7 Try again 8–16 Getting there 17–25 Good work 26–33 Excellent! ✓

Other influences on business

A

Choose just one answer: a, b, c or d.

1 The RAC motoring organisation is an example of a:
a) monopoly
b) pressure group
c) nationalised industry
d) local authority (1 mark)

2 The Citizens Advice Bureau gives advice mainly to:
a) owners b) directors
c) suppliers d) consumers (1 mark)

3 The level of demand for a firm's products is:
a) a social influence
b) a technological influence
c) a political influence
d) an economic influence (1 mark)

4 The 'P' in STEP analysis stands for:
a) promotion b) political
c) profit d) productivity (1 mark)

5 The government 'watchdogs' seek to:
a) make local authorities follow central government's policies
b) train government staff in the latest management theories
c) help management and unions solve any disagreements they may have
d) regulate major industries such as power and telecommunications (1 mark)

Score /5

B

Answer all parts of all questions.

1 Match each influence with the appropriate example.

Influence	Example
a) Social	i) The local authority stops a firm discharging waste
b) Political	ii) A new machine speeds up a firm's production processes
c) Economic	iii) There is a new fashion trend
d) Technological	iv) A new EU directive comes out
e) Environmental	v) The government adopts a 'buy British' policy
f) Legal	vi) There is a change in the base rate of interest

(6 marks)

2 Classify each of the following.

	Pressure group	Employers' association	Trade union
a) Action on Smoking and Health (ASH)	☐	☐	☐
b) UNISON	☐	☐	☐
c) Confederation of British Industry (CBI)	☐	☐	☐
d) National Association of Head Teachers	☐	☐	☐
e) Friends of the Earth	☐	☐	☐

(5 marks)

Score /11

C

These are GCSE-style questions. Answer all parts of the questions. Continue on a separate sheet where necessary.

1 ***Kemikals plc*** **manufactures chemical products. Its main plant is on the coast. The prevailing winds blow the smoke from the plant out to sea, but sometimes it is blown inland. Members of the local community are concerned that the smoke from *Kemikals plc* is harmful to the environment. The directors of *Kemikals plc* realise that any change in how they manufacture the chemicals, in order to reduce the smoke and smell, will add to their costs.**

a) Explain how members of the local community might set about taking action.

....

.... **(3 marks)**

b) Outline the possible effect on *Kemikals plc* if the local community is successful in making the company change its manufacturing processes.

....

.... **(4 marks)**

2 ***Recordit plc*** **has developed a new recordable 'hard disc' player that carries out the same function as a video recorder, but which is technologically more efficient. The company has received some government support for its research, because the government wants UK businesses to remain competitive and innovative. The company has carried out some market research, and the directors wish to market this product. They are convinced that there is an increasing trend towards 'home entertainment'. To develop and market this item further, the company will need to take out a large loan, hopefully at a low rate of interest.**

Explain fully how STEP analysis features in the above information.

....

....

....

....

....

....

....

....**(12 marks)**

Score /19

For more on this topic see pages 36–37 of your Success Guide.

Total score /35

How well did you do? ✗ 0–7 Try again 8–17 Getting there 18–27 Good work 28–35 Excellent! ✓

Employing staff

A

Choose just one answer: a, b, c or d.

1 People applying for jobs complete:

a) a person specification
b) a job description
c) an application form
d) a statement of account (1 mark)

2 A new member of staff will receive:

a) an account
b) a contract
c) an enquiry
d) a franchise (1 mark)

3 'CV' stands for:

a) curriculum vitae
b) cost variance
c) computer virus
d) credit value (1 mark)

4 One way to recruit internally is to:

a) advertise in a Job Centre
b) put a notice on the staff notice board
c) place an advert in the local paper
d) use a specialist magazine (1 mark)

5 People who are selected for interview are placed on a:

a) waiting list
b) shopping list
c) long list
d) short list (1 mark)

Score /5

B

Answer all parts of all questions.

1 Complete these sentences choosing the correct word from the box below.

When recruiting new staff, Human Resource Management staff ask interested people to complete the firm's .... form. Sometimes .... tests are used at the interview. The new employee will receive a job ...., which sets out responsibilities and duties.

description	retention	application	specification	selection	reservation

(3 marks)

2 Classify these as advantages or disadvantages of internal recruitment:

a) The person promoted is already known advantage/disadvantage

b) It may cause resentment among other staff advantage/disadvantage

c) Morale amongst staff might improve advantage/disadvantage

d) It is less expensive than external recruitment advantage/disadvantage

e) There will be a smaller choice of applicants advantage/disadvantage (5 marks)

Score /8

C

These are GCSE-style questions. Answer all parts of the questions. Continue on a separate sheet where necessary.

1 ***Barkers Ltd* makes toys for pets. The company needs to recruit a Personal Assistant for a director. The Human Resources department has written a job description and a person specification.**

a) Describe the difference between a person specification and a job description.

....

.... (2 marks)

b) Explain why it is necessary for a person specification to be written for this post.

....

.... (2 marks)

c) Name two appropriate methods to use for notifying the existing staff of *Barkers Ltd* about this vacancy.

....

.... (2 marks)

d) The short-listed candidates will be interviewed. Assess the value to *Barkers Ltd* of using interviews to select a Personal Assistant.

....

.... (4 marks)

2 ***Barkers Ltd* has recently established its own website, and needs to appoint an information and communications technology (ICT) specialist.**

a) Suggest two appropriate external methods the company should use to recruit this specialist. Justify your choice of methods.

....

.... (4 marks)

b) Explain two advantages that external recruitment has over internal recruitment when recruiting for a post such as this.

....

.... (4 marks)

Score /18

For more on this topic see pages 40–41 of your Success Guide.

Total score /31

How well did you do? ✗ 0–6 Try again 7–15 Getting there 16–25 Good work 26–31 Excellent! ✓

Training and developing staff

A

Choose just one answer: a, b, c or d.

1 The first training a member of staff receives is called:

a) induction
b) selection
c) on-the-job
d) off-the-job (1 mark)

2 One benefit to a firm of off-the-job training is that there is no disruption to:

a) pricing
b) production
c) promotion
d) purchasing (1 mark)

3 Assessing the effectiveness of an employee is called:

a) appraisal b) aptitude
c) appropriation d) automation (1 mark)

4 The skills of a workforce can be improved through:

a) advertising
b) franchising
c) training
d) selecting (1 mark)

5 Off-the-job training is most likely to be provided by a:

a) local authority
b) further education college
c) competitor
d) trade union (1 mark)

Score /5

B

Answer all parts of all questions.

1 Identify which of the following relate to on-the-job training.

	True	False
a) It focuses exclusively on the firm's needs	☐	☐
b) It is conducted by outside specialists	☐	☐
c) It takes place in a specialist training organisation	☐	☐
d) The trainer may not be highly skilled in training	☐	☐
e) It often leads to new ideas being brought into the firm	☐	☐

(5 marks)

2 Delete the incorrect word or phrase in the following sentences.

a) Training is important to businesses, because staff should be as productive/non-productive as possible. This will help a business meet its objectives/investment. Staff also benefit from training: for example, it may help them gain demotion/promotion. (3 marks)

b) Induction training is designed for the new employee/existing employee. It will ensure this employee makes a meaningful contribution to the work of the business as quickly as possible/as slowly as possible. (2 marks)

Score /10

C

These are GCSE-style questions. Answer all parts of the questions. Continue on a separate sheet where necessary.

1 ***SK Ltd* is a company that makes furniture. Its departments include Production, Sales, Finance and Human Resources. All new staff receive a week's induction training, organised by Human Resources staff.**

Outline the possible content of an induction training programme offered by *SK Ltd*.

....

....

....

....

.... **(6 marks)**

2 **After induction training, staff at *SK Ltd* receive on-the-job training.**

a) Explain two advantages to the employees of having on-the-job training.

....

.... **(4 marks)**

b) i) Explain three advantages to *SK Ltd* if the company changed to off-the-job training.

....

....

.... **(6 marks)**

ii) Give two reasons why the employees of *SK Ltd* might prefer off-the-job training.

....

.... **(4 marks)**

Score /20

For more on this topic see pages 42–43 of your Success Guide.

Total score /35

How well did you do? ✗ 0–6 Try again 7–16 Getting there 17–26 Good work 27–35 Excellent! ✓

Theories on motivating staff

A

Choose just one answer: a, b, c or d.

1 Highly motivated staff are more likely to:
a) leave the business
b) achieve business goals
c) need training
d) seek voluntary redundancy **(1 mark)**

2 Douglas McGregor wrote about:
a) hygiene factors and motivators
b) basic and safety needs
c) Theory X and Theory Y
d) satisfiers and dissatisfiers **(1 mark)**

3 An example of meeting a social need at work is:
a) holding a meeting
b) fitting a guard to a machine
c) repairing a heating unit
d) promoting a member of staff **(1 mark)**

4 Hygiene factors were explained by:
a) Abraham Maslow
b) Elton Mayo
c) Frederick Herzberg
d) Douglas McGregor **(1 mark)**

5 The number of levels in Maslow's hierarchy of needs is:
a) 3
b) 4
c) 5
d) 6 **(1 mark)**

Score /5

B

Answer all parts of all questions.

1 Reorganise these five levels into their correct order.

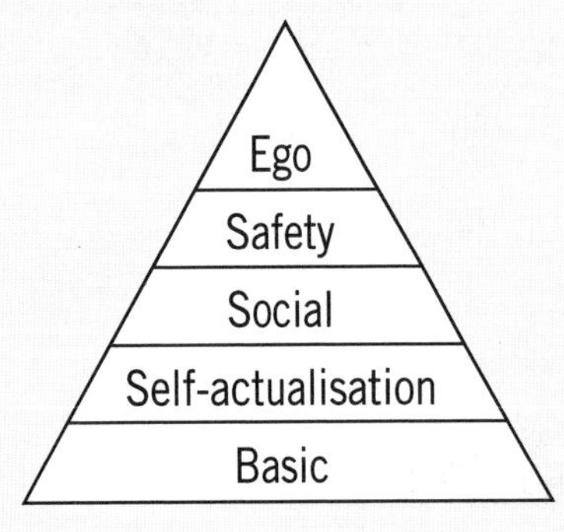

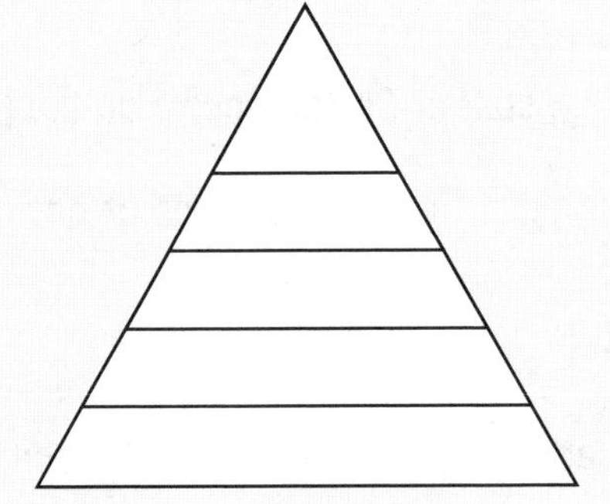

(5 marks)

2 Match the level with its most appropriate work-based example.

Level	Example
a) Self-actualisation	i) Toilets
b) Safety (security)	ii) A staff evening 'do'
c) Social	iii) Employees who have complete job satisfaction
d) Ego (esteem)	iv) Creating a redundancy pay agreement
e) Basic	v) Being made 'employee of the month'

(5 marks)

Score /10

C

These are GCSE-style questions. Answer all parts of the questions. Continue on a separate sheet where necessary.

1 **Stan and Ollie run a successful partnership, owning a number of shops that sell DVDs and computer games. Each shop has its own manager. Suggest different financial and non-financial approaches that Stan and Ollie could use to motivate their managers to increase sales.**

....

....

....

.... **(8 marks)**

STAN & OLLIES
GAMES AND MOVIES
OPEN

2 **Beryl employs staff in *Hair Today*, her hairdressing salon. Beryl believes that the only 'proper' way to motivate her staff is to offer them more pay.**

a) To what extent do the following motivation theorists agree with Beryl's view?

i) Abraham Maslow: ....

....

.... **(4 marks)**

ii) Douglas McGregor: ....

....

.... **(4 marks)**

b) Give two examples of 'hygiene factors', and two examples of 'motivators', that are likely to be present in the work of Hair Today.

....

....

....

.... **(4 marks)**

Score /20

For more on this topic see pages 44–45 of your Success Guide. Total score /35

How well did you do? ✗ 0–6 Try again 7–16 Getting there 17–26 Good work 27–35 Excellent! ✓

Paying staff

A

Choose just one answer: a, b, c or d.

1 People paid an annual fixed income receive a:
a) debenture
b) salary
c) dividend
d) wage (1 mark)

2 Pay that is based on the number of items made is known as:
a) payment by results
b) Pay As You Earn
c) pay round
d) payroll (1 mark)

3 Staff being 'paid by results' are on a:
a) flat rate system
b) time rate system
c) piece rate system
d) bonus (1 mark)

4 Offering staff cheap or free company shares is called:
a) a profit sharing scheme
b) a share-out scheme
c) a share premium scheme
d) a share ownership scheme (1 mark)

5 Under a 'flat rate' system, an employee receives:
a) a fixed amount for work done
b) an agreed amount for every hour worked
c) a merit bonus for work done
d) a flat to live in (1 mark)

Score /5

B

Answer all parts of the question.

1 Here is an extract from a job advertisement. Explain the terms underlined in the advertisement.

Shop manager
required for busy town centre shop.

Basic salary £18 000

plus commission and
company benefits

the company operates a
profit-sharing scheme

The successful applicant will be expected to work overtime in busy periods.

For further details, please write to:

PO BOX 121
Jobstown
Staffordshire

Basic salary: ....

Commission: ....

Company benefits: ....

Profit-sharing scheme: ....

Overtime: .... (10 marks)

Score /10

C

These are GCSE-style questions. Answer all parts of the questions. Continue on a separate sheet where necessary.

1 **Explain one advantage and one disadvantage to a business of paying its sales staff by fixed salary.**

....

.... (4 marks)

2 **As well as paying salaries to their employees, many businesses offer benefits such as profit sharing or staff discounts.**

a) Explain why a business may offer each of these benefits to its staff.

Profit sharing: ....

....

Staff discounts: ....

.... (4 marks)

b) Name two other benefits a major retailer such as *Sainsbury's* or *Tesco* might offer its staff.

....

.... (2 marks)

3 ***Writewell Ltd*** **is a publishing company. Staff working in its offices receive a salary, and staff in the printing department are paid a wage. Sales staff, who sell the company's books to retailers such as** ***WH Smith*****, receive a bonus if they reach an agreed sales target. The company pays its authors a percentage commission on the number of books sold.**

a) Describe three likely differences between wages and salaries at *Writewell Ltd.*

....

....

.... (6 marks)

b) Describe two likely differences between bonuses and commission at *Writewell Ltd.*

....

.... (4 marks)

Score /20

For more on this topic see pages 46–47 of your Success Guide.

Total score /35

How well did you do? ✗ 0–6 Try again 7–16 Getting there 17–26 Good work 27–35 Excellent! ✓

Groups in business

A

Choose just one answer: a, b, c or d.

1 Local people who object to the activities of a business may join together and form a:

a) hierarchy
b) trade union
c) pressure group
d) company **(1 mark)**

2 An option for staff who are in dispute with their employer is:

a) nationalisation
b) negotiation
c) negligence
d) networking **(1 mark)**

3 The Musicians' Union is an example of:

a) a craft union
b) an industrial union
c) a general union
d) white collar union **(1 mark)**

4 'TUC' stands for:

a) Trades Union Congress
b) Trades Union Council
c) Trades United Congress
d) Trades United Council **(1 mark)**

5 An example of an employers' association is the:

a) National Union of Journalists
b) TUC
c) Department of Social Security
d) Road Haulage Association **(1 mark)**

Score /5

B

Answer all parts of all questions.

1 Delete the incorrect word or phrase in the following sentences.

A trade union seeks to support/train its members by arguing/negotiating with employers. Examples of union aims/leaders include seeking to lengthen the hours/improve the pay of members, protecting their jobs/houses, and improving living/working conditions. **(6 marks)**

2 Match each term or phrase with the correct description.

Term/Phrase	Description
a) Affiliated	i) A person representing union members at the workplace
b) Industrial union	ii) A group representing employers
c) Shop steward	iii) The organisation for a specific group of workers
d) The CBI	iv) Discussions to improve pay levels
e) Wage negotiations	v) Joined together with others

(5 marks)

Score /11

C

These are GCSE-style questions. Answer all parts of the questions. Continue on a separate sheet where necessary.

1 a) Give three examples of the normal activities of a trade union in the workplace.

....

....

.... (3 marks)

b) Union membership has fallen in the last 20 years. Suggest two reasons for this.

....

.... (2 marks)

c) Erica is a member of a trade union that represents staff in the public sector. She has been involved in an accident at work. Describe how Erica's union might assist her in this matter.

....

....

....

.... (4 marks)

2 **Oliver Smith is a famous chef who runs several restaurants in London. Smith employs many cooks and other staff in his restaurants. These employees work long hours and are not well paid. Smith does not encourage his staff to become members of a trade union, although several of them do belong to different unions.**

a) Suggest three ways in which being members of a single trade union might help Smith's staff.

....

....

....

....

....

.... (6 marks)

b) Outline the advantages and disadvantages to Smith of his staff being represented by a single union.

....

....

....

.... (4 marks)

Score /19

For more on this topic see pages 48–49 of your Success Guide.

Total score /35

How well did you do? ✗ 0–6 Try again 7–16 Getting there 17-25 Good work 26–35 Excellent! ✓

Working together

A

Choose just one answer: a, b, c or d.

1 Negotiation between unions and employers is called:

a) collective bargaining
b) code of practice
c) business planning
d) double-entry bookkeeping **(1 mark)**

2 An example of industrial action is:

a) works council
b) work measurement
c) work-to-rule
d) work shadowing **(1 mark)**

3 Settling disputes is often achieved through the work of:

a) ASCA
b) ACAS
c) CASA
d) ASAC **(1 mark)**

4 A 'single-union' agreement is when:

a) only single people can join the union
b) new members must join one at a time
c) the employer only recognises one union
d) there has only ever been one union in the factory **(1 mark)**

5 A union strike requires a:

a) budget
b) brand
c) balance
d) ballot **(1 mark)**

Score /5

B

Answer all parts of all questions.

1 Match each type of dispute to the correct description.

Name	Description
a) Overtime ban	i) Union members withdraw their labour
b) Work-to-rule	ii) Members follow all procedures 'to the letter'
c) Go-slow	iii) Members stand outside to persuade others not to attend
d) Sit-in	iv) Members only work their normal hours
e) Strike	v) Members occupy the firm's buildings
f) Picketing	vi) Members carry out their work more slowly than normal

(6 marks)

2 Complete the sentences below:

The main services offered by ACAS are:

- C.. – an ACAS official discusses the d.. with both parties.
- AC.. – the parties in dispute agree to accept the ruling of an i.. t.. p..

(4 marks)

Score /10

Letts

GCSE Success

Workbook Answer Booklet

Business Studies

David Floyd

Answer Booklet

GCSE Business Studies

OUR ECONOMY

Our economy

A
1 b 2 c 3 a 4 c 5 c

B
1 The corrected links are: labour and wages; enterprise and profits
2 The links are: a with iv and 2; b with ii and 1; c with i and 4; d with iii and 3

C
1 a) Reduced costs, e.g. through training and efficiency; increased quality through reliable and accurate machines.
b) Employees become bored as a result of repetitive jobs, leading to higher labour turnover.
2 a) Staff (labour); loans (capital); display equipment (capital).
b) Competitors: are their prices higher or lower? Quality: do they provide good-quality foodstuffs?
c) Jane and John follow the 'division of labour' principle. This allows each to specialise, making the business more efficient.

Types of economy

A
1 d 2 c 3 b 4 b 5 b

B
1 Goods: shampoo, towels, car and petrol; the hairdresser and garage provide a service.
2 The gaps are (in order): profit motive; what; where; how; private; public; profit; service.

C
1 Maximising profit: obtaining as much profit as possible. Survival: staying in business. Increasing market share: selling a greater percentage of the value of the products in that market than before.
2 The links are: i with e; ii with g; iii with c; iv with d.
3 Private sector: the sector of the economy where individuals can set up in business with a view to making profits. Public sector: the sector that is controlled by the state, which provides necessary services.

Locating business

A
1 b 2 c 3 d 4 d 5 a

B
1 a, b, f
2 insurance; banking; transport.

C
1 a) tertiary
b) primary
2 Existing skills and loyalty; pay levels in the new area may be much higher.
3 a) Costs: what costs are involved? Staff: will the staff want to move?
b) Arranging the move; obtaining premises, etc; persuading staff to move; informing customers and suppliers.
c) Employment opportunities: greater or fewer? Property prices: how will these be affected?

The European Union

A
1 c 2 a 3 b 4 d 5 c

B
1 The percentages are: 10% to the rest of the world; 11% to Asia and Oceania; 14% to North and South America; 65% to the EU.
2 If the UK joins the Eurozone, exchange rate fluctuations will no longer take place. Price differences between countries will be easier to see because all goods and services will be valued in euros.

C
1 Advantages: easier to compare prices when buying items; only dealing in a single currency. Disadvantages: price 'transparency' may indicate the UK business is uncompetitive; still need to cope with a changing euro–pound exchange rate.
2 a) i) Free movement of people and goods, and common standards.
ii) CE marking; controlling mergers; protecting consumers.
b) Directives and regulations; finance (loans).
c) Marketing, e.g. different language for labels and adverts. Finance: handling the euro. Human resources: training staff to deal with overseas business.

International business

A
1 a 2 b 3 a 4 d 5 a

B
1 The links are: a with i and 2; b with ii and 1.
2 Benefits of exporting: a, b and e; benefits of importing: c and d.

C
1 a) *Pushkids:* greater sales mean possible economies of scale. Customers: lower prices as a result of economies of scale.
b) Need to check safety and other requirements; need to check different cultural and other habits; problems of changing their marketing strategy and content (e.g. foreign language).
c) Any of the three could be selected. Arguments include: Ireland – in EU; uses the euro; fewer export formalities; same language but the lowest population. France – in EU; uses the euro; fewer export formalities; larger market than Ireland but different language. USA – the largest market; the richest market; the same language but furthest away; not in EU so more export formalities; uses the dollar.

Sole trader and partnership businesses

A
1 d 2 b 3 a 4 d 5 a

B
1 i) easier ii) harder iii) can
2 Sole trader: a, c and f; partnership: d and e; both: b (and f).

C
1 a) She may have to use her personal wealth to repay business debts because a sole trader has unlimited liability.
b) i) They can specialise in different aspects of the business (e.g. Rashid in marketing). More capital is likely to be available.
ii) She has to share profits with Rashid. She will need to consult with him over major business decisions.
c) They have limited liability, so they will not have to use personal resources to meet business debts.
d) How they share any profits/losses; how much each invests in the business; how business disputes are to be settled.

Limited companies

A
1 d 2 d 3 a 4 d 5 b

B
1 Sole trader: d and f; partnership: b; limited company: a, c and e.
2 Compared with plcs, a private limited company is less likely to suffer from 'red tape' because it is normally much smaller. The shares of a private company cannot be traded on the Stock Exchange. As a result, it is less likely to be the subject of a hostile takeover bid.

C
1 a) Shareholders
b) Limited liability
c) Secondary sector
d) Mass production
e) Stock Exchange
2 Shareholders are more interested in short-term profits and dividend payments, whereas directors tend to look more to the long term (e.g. business growth). Shareholders and directors therefore often have differing business objectives. Shareholders are owners of the business; directors may have shares (so may be owners) but are more involved with controlling it.
3 Limited liability: they will no longer risk losing their personal wealth if the business owes debts it cannot pay. Continuity: if either dies or leaves, the business can continue in its own right. Finance: limited companies often find loans are easier (and cheaper) to obtain.

Other businesses

A
1 d 2 b 3 c 4 a 5 a

B
1 The company that awards a franchise is called the franchisor, and the person who takes on this franchise is known as a franchisee. The franchising company supplies the product and expertise, and in return receives capital.
2 a) true b) true
c) false d) true
e) false f) false

C
1 a) Advantages: a known product; expert support. Disadvantages: has to provide capital; will have to pay a royalty or fee to *Dave's DVDs.*
b) There is no need to provide the capital to expand; the franchisee will be highly motivated to make the business successful.
2 a) Multinational company: a business with its HQ in one country, and operations in other countries. Public corporation: state-owned industries that supply goods and services for the benefit of the public.
b) Advantages: new processes and techniques are introduced; higher employment. Disadvantages: profits may be taken out of the country; the multinational may be able to avoid paying UK tax.
c) Natural monopolies, such as water, can be closely regulated; national security (defence issues) is under state control.

Stakeholders in business

A
1 b 2 d 3 c 4 b 5 d

B
1 The links are: a with i; b with iv; c with ii; d with iii.
2 The links are: a with iv; b with i; c with ii; d with iii.

C
1 a) i) To expand by entering different markets.
ii) The children's farm; the craft shop centre.
iii) The company is more likely to survive; it should increase its profits.
b) i) Survival is a more appropriate aim, although Lee could grow through diversifying into other artistic areas, e.g. sculpture.
ii) This objective could be fully appropriate; diversification would be different to *Eatwell's*, e.g. by entering export markets.
iii) Inappropriate for DEFRA because it has a specific focus; its key objectives are likely to be service-based, e.g. to do with public confidence in food.

INSIDE AND OUTSIDE THE BUSINESS

The main functions of business

A
1 b 2 d 3 a 4 d 5 c

B
1 Carrying out market research; advertising products.
2 The links are: a with iv; b with i; c with ii; d with iii.

C
1 a) Finance handles the company's money – recording, receiving, and paying – and calculates its profit and financial position.
b) Marketing is responsible for helping the company sell its products as efficiently as possible.
c) Production manufactures the products that Marketing sells.
2 a) Staff appraisal; recruitment and selection; dismissal; staff records.
b) i) Induction: offered to new recruits. On-the-job: training in the company, often by staff who do the job. Off-the-job: training externally, using specialist training providers.
ii) Off-the-job.
c) Job: one-off production, designed to meet individual requirements. Batch: producing a limited number of identical products.

Organising business

A
1 c 2 b 3 a 4 c 5 d

B
1 a)

Board of directors
Managing Director
Purchasing Manager | Sales Manager | Accounts Manager | Human Resources Manager

b) The links are: i with 3; ii with 4; iii with 2; iv with 1.

C
1 a) i) The number of staff under the direct control of a superior.
ii) The chain through which information and control passes.
iii) The structure of an organisation.
b) One (Accounts Manager).
c) The Production Director.
d) It confirms the authority and responsibility of staff. It can be used in induction training to help new staff understand the structure of the business.
e) Authority means the formal power to command others to do something, e.g. the HR Director has the authority to make the Staff Welfare Manager arrange or carry out certain staff training. Responsibility is associated with making decisions or getting results, e.g. the Staff Welfare Manager is responsible for the work his/her staff do. Accountability means the extent to which one person is responsible for his/her actions, e.g. the Staff Welfare Manager is accountable to the HR Director.

Communicating in business

A
1 a 2 d 3 a 4 d 5 c

B
1 The correct order is: 1e buyer to seller; 2f seller to buyer; 3c buyer to seller; 4b seller to buyer; 5h seller to buyer; 6a seller to buyer; 7g seller to buyer; 8d buyer to seller.
2 Items not appearing are: details of income tax; amount of profit; last month's amount owed; previous payments made; cheque number.

C
1 a) So her accountant can regularly inform Jackie face-to-face about her financial position; Jackie can ask questions and get answers.
b) So the accountant can explain to Jackie how profitable her business has been, how much tax she owes, and when she will have to pay it.
2 a) Memos are an internal communication method; they are less formal.
b) E-mail: attachments can be sent; it is immediate; figures can be written out accurately; the sender doesn't know if the recipient has read it. Telephone: it is direct; the sender knows the message is received; the sender can explain things; the figures may be copied down wrongly; there is no official written record.
c) It motivates staff, who feel more involved in the business; it informs staff about any current developments.

How a business grows

A
1 c 2 c 3 a 4 c 5 c

B
1 The links are: a with iv; b with iii; c with i; d with ii.
2 a) organic b) vertical
c) horizontal d) lateral
e) organic f) horizontal

C
1 a) Enter the business accommodation market; convert the storerooms to bedrooms.
b) They have no spare capital, and borrowing might be expensive. They may also lack cash to advertise more, or to advertise using different media.
c) i) They may gain from economies of scale. Also, if they gain customers by word of mouth about their good personal service, business will increase.
ii) They may suffer from diseconomies of scale. They may cease to be able to provide the personal service on which their reputation is based, because they are too busy.
d) They could compare the position a year ago in terms of: the number of staff hours employed; the amount of capital employed in the business; the average number of rooms booked (percentage occupied) each day; the amount of net profit they make.

Supporting business

A
1 c 2 a 3 a 4 a 5 d

B
1

C
1 a) The ONS prepares and publishes a range of statistics on behalf of the UK government.
b) UK Trade & Investment provides information and support to UK exporters.
c) ECGD insures certain UK businesses against losses when exporting.
2 To remain competitive internationally; to help provide employment in the UK.
3 It has removed trade barriers between EU countries, so UK businesses can have full access to a huge market.
4 a) Advice on all business aspects; grants, loans, and loan guarantees; statistics to help decision-making; legal protection; support to help train staff; support and advice if Jim decides to export.
b) Advice and information, e.g. on documents required and on dealing with other EU countries; possible financial assistance, e.g. grants.

Business and the law

A
1 d 2 b 3 b 4 b 5 c

B
1 The links are: a with iv; b with vi; c with ii; d with v; e with i; f with iii.
2 a) false b) true
c) false d) true

C
1 Price indication: goods must show full details of prices. Misleading advertising: adverts must not mislead. CE marking: this safety mark can only be added to products meeting a given safety standard.
2 a) Sale and Supply of Goods; Rachel can take the item back and get a refund (the item is not of satisfactory quality).
b) Sale and Supply of Goods (you might also argue Trade Descriptions here); David can change the item (the item is not as described).
c) Health and Safety at Work; the employer will take action against them (employees must take reasonable care of themselves and others).

d) Equal Pay: Jayne should get £5.50 per hour (employees should receive the same pay for the same work).

Other influences on business

A

1 b 2 d 3 d 4 b 5 d

B

1 The links are: a with iii; b with v; c with vi; d with ii; e with i; f with iv.
2 All five (especially a and e) are pressure groups; c is also an employers' association; b and d are unions.

C

1 a) They could form a pressure group since they have the same interest and need a single voice to represent them. Group leaders could then meet with the company's management.
b) If the company changes its production processes, these may make its chemicals more expensive to produce, and less competitive compared with their rivals' products. As a result, the company may lose sales and become less profitable.
2 Social: the company's market research suggests that there is a growth in home entertainment in the UK. Technological: the new player is technologically more efficient than a video recorder. Economic: the company wants to borrow money, but will need to check the current interest rates to see if it can afford the loan. Political: the government has supported the company in its research into hard disc recorders.

PEOPLE IN BUSINESS

Employing staff

A

1 c 2 b 3 a 4 b 5 d

B

1 When recruiting new staff, Human Resource Management staff ask interested people to complete the firm's application form. Sometimes selection tests are used at the interview. The new employee will receive a job description, which sets out responsibilities and duties.
2 Advantages: a, c, d; disadvantages: b, e.

C

1 a) Person specification: outlines the personal skills and abilities needed to do the job. Job description: outlines the duties and responsibilities of the job.
b) So interviewers can more fully assess applicants; so applicants are aware whether they have the necessary qualities.
c) Staff notice board; staff magazine.
d) Interviews are two-way, allowing applicants the opportunity to see the company and ask questions, and interviewers to ask applicants about their background, why they want the job, and so on. However, they are time-consuming and can therefore be expensive.
2 a) Specialist ICT magazine: it reaches the target market. JobCentre or other employment agency: they will have specialist ICT staff 'on their books' looking for jobs.
b) New expertise is brought into the firm, which can improve its efficiency. There is a wider choice of applicants, which may well result in a better applicant being appointed.

Training and developing staff

A

1 a 2 b 3 a 4 c 5 b

B

1 a) true b) false
c) false d) true
e) false
2 a) Training is important to businesses, because staff should be as productive as possible. This will help a business meet its objectives. Staff also benefit from training, for example, it may help them gain promotion.
b) Induction training is designed for the new employee. It will ensure this employee makes a meaningful contribution to the work of the business as quickly as possible.

C

1 History of the company; the company's present position in its market; role of each department; tour of the premises; meet your manager; meet your department staff.
2 a) It is specific training, devoted entirely to their needs; they feel as though they are making an immediate contribution to the work of the company.
b) i) The quality of the training may improve (specialist trainers). The training becomes more focused, and new ideas are likely to be brought into the company from outside. The training may be less expensive, e.g. employees carry it out in their own time.
ii) The employees are away from work pressures, and are therefore more relaxed. They may receive an external certificate or diploma, which they regard as valuable.

Theories on motivating staff

A

1 b 2 c 3 a 4 c 5 c

B

1

Self-actualisation
Ego
Social
Safety
Basic

2 The links are: a with iii; b with iv; c with ii; d with v; e with i.

C

1 Financial: bonus if a certain sales total is reached; commission on each sale made; profit-sharing if a profit target is reached.
Non-financial: improved working conditions; time off if a certain target is met; training schemes.
2 a) i) Maslow accepts that pay is important (e.g. his 'security' level), but also that there are other motivating factors at work that may not be related to pay, notably job satisfaction.
ii) McGregor's Theory Y person seeks responsibility, and is not solely motivated by pay. McGregor believed that people are not exclusively motivated by pay levels.
b) Hygiene factors: salary, rest breaks. Motivators: having the quality of the employee's work recognised (e.g. customer praise), and when an employee is given more responsibility.

Paying staff

A

1 b 2 a 3 c 4 d 5 a

B

1 Basic salary: the minimum amount paid for the year. Commission: earnings over basic salary, e.g. based on sales. Company benefits: examples include a company car, pension scheme, subsidised meals. Profit-sharing scheme: if a profits target is met, staff share some of the excess profits. Overtime: time worked and paid for over and above the number of hours agreed in the contract of employment.

C

1 Advantage: the company knows its salary costs in advance, so can budget accurately. Disadvantage: there is no motivation for the staff to work harder, so sales may not increase.
2 a) Profit sharing: to encourage staff to work hard, so profits will increase and all gain; labour turnover is likely to be low. Discounts: may be a less expensive incentive than increasing pay; helps recruitment, and encourages loyalty amongst existing staff.
b) Share ownership; subsidised travel to and from work.
3 a) Wages are paid weekly, salaries monthly. Wages may vary, salaries are fixed. Wages are associated with manual work, salaries with clerical work.
b) Bonuses may be paid once a year, commission much more frequently. Bonuses may be fixed or variable, commission is variable.

Groups in business

A

1 c 2 b 3 a 4 a 5 d

B

1 A trade union seeks to support its members by negotiating with employers. Examples of union aims include seeking to improve the pay of members, protecting their jobs, and improving working conditions.
2 The links are: a with v; b with iii; c with i; d with ii; e with iv.

C

1 a) Negotiate to improve pay levels; seek to improve safety; support employees through giving advice.
b) A switch from the traditional manufacturing base (traditionally union-based) to a tertiary-based economy; a reduction in the power of unions as a result of government legislation.
c) The union will give legal and other advice to Erica; it will represent her at any discussions with the firm's management; it may take the case to an industrial tribunal, and represent her at the tribunal.
2 a) They have greater power in wage and other negotiations through being represented by a single body; they receive the same information and protection, so no one person is disadvantaged; they may have greater involvement in any decision-making through union representation.

b) Advantages: only having to deal with a single body that represents his staff. Disadvantages: Smith may end up paying higher wages than if he negotiated with workers individually.

Working together

A

1 a 2 c 3 b 4 c 5 d

B

1 The links are: a with iv; b with ii; c with vi; d with v; e with i; f with iii.
2 Conciliation – an ACAS official discusses the dispute with both parties. Arbitration – the parties in dispute agree to accept the ruling of an independent third party.

C

1 It listens to both sides of the employer–employee dispute, and makes a judgement in favour of one of these parties. Its judgement may involve reinstating the employee, or giving the employee financial compensation, if it considers the employee has been treated unfairly.
2 a) Trade union: a group of employees who unite to negotiate with employers. Shop steward: an unpaid union representative in the workplace. Collective bargaining: official negotiations between employers and unions. In dispute: the union disagrees with some policy of the employer, and takes some form of action.
b) Employees will be affected financially, by losing pay. They may also find that there are fewer work opportunities after the strike, if the firm has lost a lot of business. The employers will lose production, and may lose markets and the goodwill of their customers.
c) ACAS may offer to conciliate, with one of its officials discussing the dispute with both sides. ACAS may offer to arbitrate, acting as an independent 'judge' in the dispute and making a decision that both parties have agreed they will accept.

FINANCE IN BUSINESS

Finance for business

A

1 d 2 a 3 a 4 b 5 a

B

1 Internal sources: b, c, f, g; external sources: a, d, e.
2 a) A public limited company can advertise its shares for sale to the general public.
b) Ordinary shares normally carry a vote. These shares receive a dividend.
c) Debenture holders are lenders to a company. Debentures receive interest.

C

1 It avoids paying interest, and is therefore cheaper. There is no need to negotiate a loan, and no concerns about providing security. However, retained profits use cash already inside the business, which might leave the business short of cash in the future.
2 a) Arthur and Brian: overdraft, which is flexible, and they only need pay interest on the amount overdrawn. Chen: long-term bank loan, for a fixed term, and based on the amount that has to be paid for the lorry. Diane: trade credit, which will enable her to save cash that she can then use to finance the redecoration.
b) The type of project is different in each case; the nature of the business and the degree of risk to the lender also vary.
3 a) Provide advice: a bank can give specialist help. Provide an overdraft: this is a flexible and short-term method of borrowing, suitable for buying extra stock.
b) Trade credit benefits the business because suppliers are helping to finance the stock. *PDG Ltd* may be able to buy the stock, sell it, and use the cash to repay the suppliers.

Financial records in business 1

A

1 d 2 b 3 c 4 a 5 c

B

1 A trading profit and loss account contains information on revenues, expenses, gross and net profit. A balance sheet shows details of a business's assets, liabilities and capital.
2

	£000	£000
Sales		755
Cost of goods sold		100
Gross profit		655
Interest received		5
Other income		25
		685
Interest paid	45	
Salaries	240	
Rent and rates	60	
Other expenses	70	415
Net profit		270

C

1 a) turnover
b) materials (e.g. cases); labour (wages)
c) i) current assets
ii) current liabilities
iii) current assets
iv) long-term liabilities
v) capital and reserves
d) profit is net sales less total expenses = £900 000
e) balance sheet of *Good Sounds Ltd*:

	£000	£000
Fixed assets		4000
Current assets	1500	
Less		
Current liabilities	(1000)	500
Less		
Long-term liabilities		(2500)
		2000
Capital and reserves		2000

f) i) Working capital is current assets less current liabilities = £500 000
ii) The company may not be able to meet its short-term debts (e.g. pay its suppliers), which means it will have to borrow money. This will add to its costs (it must pay interest) and reduce its profits.

Financial records in business 2

A

1 a 2 a 3 a 4 b 5 d

B

1 a) expense b) liability
c) liability d) asset
e) revenue f) expense.
2 It is the role of financial accounting to collect financial information from original documents such as invoices. This information is recorded in the accounts, and it can then be analysed by the accountant. The accountant will then communicate this information to other managers.

C

1 a) Missing figures are:
A £16 250 B £41 250
C £17 250 D £24 000
b) His net profit figure indicates how much he has made, and has to live on, from his business. It is a more important indicator of his profitability, when compared with his investment in the business. It is the figure from which the tax he owes will be calculated.
c) i) Assets; liabilities.
ii) Assets: cash till, shop fittings. Liabilities: suppliers owed money; VAT owing.
iii) Dave's balance sheet.
d) Stop employing help: this may leave him short-staffed at busy times, affecting customer goodwill and future sales if customers are left waiting a long time to be served. Stop advertising: this may affect his future sales, since potential customers may not realise he is trading.

Interpreting business accounts 1

A

1 c 2 b 3 d 4 a 5 d

B

1

	£000	£000
Sales		750
Opening stock	25	
Add purchases	425	
	450	
Less closing stock	30	
Cost of sales		420
Gross profit		330
Rent and rates	40	
Selling expenses	10	
Office expenses	30	
Wages and salaries	20	
Total expenses		100
Net profit		230

C

1 a) Year 1 = 16%,
Year 2 = 12%,
Year 3 = 8%.
b) First, the gross profit margin has fallen, from 40% year 1, to 38% year 2, to 36% year 3. This has a 'knock-on' effect on the net profit margin. Second, the expenses as a percentage of sales must have risen.
2 Ratios (this year's figures first): Gross profit margins: 40%, 35%; Net profit margins: 15%, 8%; Return on capital employed: 20%, 10%; Current ratios: 0.8 to 1, 1 to 1; Acid tests: 0.4 to 1, 0.6 to 1. The firm's profitability has increased substantially, and it makes 15p for every £1 of sales compared with 8p last year. It has doubled its return on capital employed, from 10p for every £1 to 20p. However, its liquidity position is much worse. Its current ratio has fallen below 1:1, and its acid test has also fallen. This means that, although it is more profitable, it may face some difficulty in meeting its short-term debts.

Interpreting business accounts 2

A

1 c 2 b 3 a 4 b 5 c

B

1 The links are: a with iv; b with i; c with ii; d with iii.
2 a) & b) current or acid test ratios (for survival);
c) & d) return on capital (to assess profitability).
3 a) right
b) wrong; gross profit margin = $\frac{\text{gross profit}}{\text{sales}} \times 100$.

C

1 a) Ratios (Laurel first):
i) 40%, 35%
ii) 20%, 15%
iii) 50%, 36%
iv) 0.75 to 1, 1.5 to 1

v) 0.5 to 1, 1 to 1
vi) 29 days, 30 days
vii) 61 days, 47 days
viii) 11.25 times in the period, 7.8 times in the period

b) Laurel has a better set of profitability ratios: the net profit and gross profit margins are both 5% higher, and there is a much higher return on capital employed (50% compared with 36%). In terms of liquidity, however, Laurel is in a weaker position. The current and acid test ratios are both lower than Hardy's. Both companies' debtors take about a month to pay, but Laurel takes 2 months to pay his creditors, compared with Hardy's 112 months. Laurel has a faster stock turnover. Overall, assuming Laurel's high creditors' payment period is not a result of a cash shortage (as suggested by its worse liquidity position), it can be said that Laurel is performing better than Hardy.

Costs in business

A
1 b 2 a 3 b 4 a 5 b

B
1 a) i) fixed ii) variable
iii) variable iv) fixed
v) fixed/variable
vi) semi-variable (probably).
b) i) indirect ii) direct
iii) direct iv) indirect
v) direct/indirect vi) indirect.
2 a) true
b) false
c) true
d) false, but may be accepted as true
e) true.

C
1 a) Fixed: rent, business rates. Variable: cost of the materials in the goods being made, cost of any wages paid on an hourly basis (e.g. shop cleaners, piece-work staff making the goods).
b) Direct: raw materials, piece-work labour on the factory floor. Indirect: business rent, shop staff salaries.
c) i) The analysis into fixed and variable costs helps the business make decisions, e.g. by calculating its break-even sales.
ii) Classifying costs as direct and indirect helps the business work out the full cost of making its products, by sharing out the indirect costs to individual products.

2 a) It can help the company set target costs: it then compares the actual costs it has paid against these targets, and can analyse them to discover the reason for any differences.
b) An opportunity cost is the 'cost of a forgone opportunity'. In this case, if the firm decides to make parts for *Vauxhall*, it loses the chance to sell parts to *Ford* and to make a profit on this.

Breaking even in business

A
1 b 2 b 3 c 4 a 5 b

B
1 a) 2500, £50 000
b) 2040, £89 760
c) 3050, £38 125
2

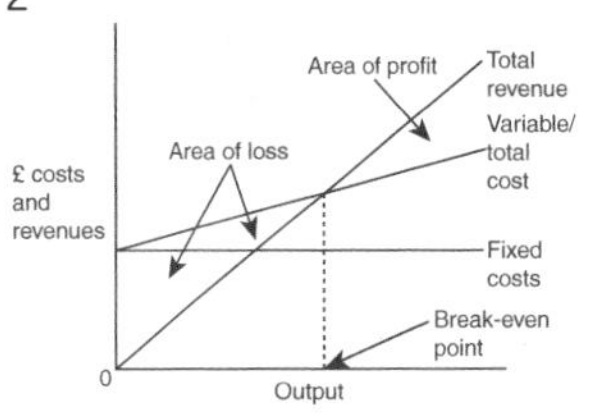

C
1 Variable costs (£): 40 000; 60 000; 80 000; 100 000; 120 000.
Total costs (£): 240 000; 260 000; 280 000; 300 000; 320 000.
Sales revenue (£): 120 000; 180 000; 240 000; 300 000; 360 000.
The break-even point is at 5 000 units (£300 000 total costs = £300 000 sales revenue).
2 Variable costs are £15 (£6 + 2 x 50p + £1 + £7), so contribution is £25 – £15 = £10. Fixed costs total £55 000 so break-even is at 5500 units (5500 x £25 = £137 500 revenue).
Margin of safety is 7500 – 5500 = 2000 units.

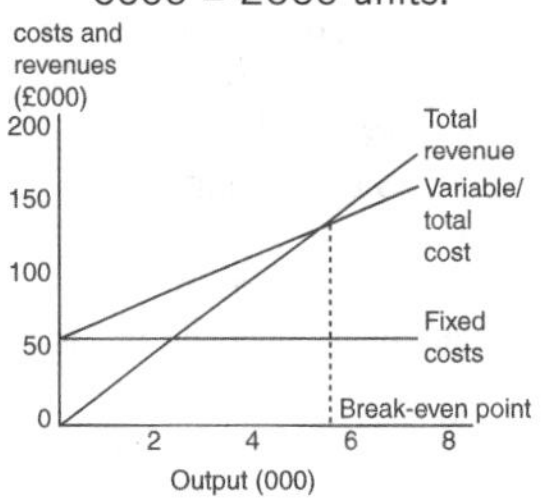

Budgeting in business

A
1 c 2 b 3 d 4 a 5 d

B
1 a) use b) source
c) source d) source
e) source f) use
g) use
2 Production; sales; raw material purchases.

C
1 There is an uncertain income (the crowd varies), so there is no guaranteed income. As a result, costs have to be carefully controlled, and setting a budget within which the manager must work is a way of controlling how much can be spent.
2 a) The missing figures are (£000): February, opening balance = 14; March, closing balance = (3) (overdrawn); April, opening balance = (3); June, cash from sales = 110.
b) i) It needs to borrow money to cover the overdrawn balance of £3 000 shown. ii) During April and May there is a high cash balance, so the company should look to invest some of this surplus for a short term.
3 a) The amount by which the cash coming in exceeds cash going out.
b) i) Actual inflow is £2900 (£18 500 – £15 600); budgeted inflow is £2000 (£18 000 – £16 000). The difference is £900.
ii) Pay is £300 higher than budget (forecast); materials cost £700 less than budget; cash sales are £1000 above budget; payments from credit customers are £500 below budget.

MAKING THE PRODUCTS

Production in business

A
1 c 2 b 3 c 4 a 5 c

B
1 a) mass b) job
c) batch d) mass
e) mass f) job
g) batch
2 Mass production, also known as continuous production, is normally associated with automation. As a result, machinery replaces people. Total costs are reduced but staff who work in a largely automated factory often become bored. Mass production depends on the product having a very high demand.

C
1 a) i) job ii) batch
b) Longer time spent making them; no economies of scale; materials will be more expensive.
2 a) Batch production (or flow-line production).
b) Machines and equipment can be organised efficiently; efficient production can lead to economies of scale.
c) Repetitive work; employees can easily become bored. Specialist work; if there is a fall in demand for these products, employees may find it hard to find another job.
d) Stockholding costs should be reduced: little stock will be held, cutting wastage and storage costs. However, the company must make sure it has a very efficient ordering and delivery system to avoid running out of stock.

Economies of scale

A
1 b 2 a 3 b 4 a 5 a

B
1 a) marketing b) technical
c) purchasing d) financial
e) managerial
2 A firm's costs can be classed as either fixed or variable. As its output increases, the firm's fixed costs will still stay at the same level. As a result, although total costs are still increasing, the average cost for each product made is falling. The cost per unit made is therefore lower. This is because the firm's fixed costs are being spread over larger output.

C
1 a) The company will gain from external economies of scale. It will gain economies of concentration (e.g. local labour is skilled in making china and pottery), of information (it may work with others in the same area, e.g. to lobby a local authority to improve roads or access), and of reputation (it will benefit from the good name for pottery and china that this area has).
b) i) Purchasing economies (e.g. buy in bulk); financial economies (e.g. obtaining loans at cheaper rates); managerial economies (e.g. employing specialists); technical economies (e.g. being able to afford modern machinery).
ii) These are hand-made: as a result, it will be difficult or impossible to use mass production methods. The level of demand for these products is not likely to be high enough to support mass production methods.
2 a) When businesses expand work may become more inefficient, which causes unit costs to rise.
b) i) Decisions will take longer to communicate,

which will mean the company is less able to respond to market and other changes.
ii) Employees will find it more difficult to carry out their work efficiently, which will affect the quality of the company's output, and therefore its sales.

c) They should review the organisational structure of *Sound Goods Ltd*, e.g. they could de-layer, because it has a tall hierarchy. This would reduce the number of levels through which information needs to flow, and should lead to wider spans of control. Managers could also train staff in good communication practice.

Productivity

A

1 b 2 b 3 d 4 c 5 a

B

1 The links are: a with iii; b with iv; c with vi; d with v; e with i; f with ii.
2 a) i
  b) ii

C

1 It is in a very competitive market, so it needs to control its costs through high productivity, otherwise it may not be able to sell its products.
2 a) Disposing of the old factory will mean that its capacity is lost. It appears that the new factory can cope with the capacity required, on its own.
  b) Fewer resources (inputs) will be used to produce the same level of production (outputs). This increases productivity.
  c) Staff: will they be prepared to travel? Will the company be able to retain the staff it wants to keep? Factory: can it be sold? Does its market price make it worth selling? The future: can the company expand in the future if sales increase, or will the new factory turn out to be too small?
  d) Staff may find it difficult to cope with their workload. Equipment may not be able to cope, breaking down, and production will be lost.

Quality and stock control

A

1 c 2 d 3 b 4 a 5 a

B

1 a) too much b) too much
  c) too little d) too little
  e) too much f) too little
2 The links are: a with iii; b with i; c with ii; d with iv.

C

1 a) Stocks held should be minimised through regular deliveries. This should mean that no (or much less) food is wasted through holding too much.
  b) Lower costs through less wastage. Less stock held, which again lowers costs.
  c) TQM seeks to 'get it right first time'. This is important to a business working in the food industry, e.g. because it needs first-class hygiene. All staff are involved in this aspect of the business, which is a key feature of TQM. A failure to get hygiene right means that customers will be affected, which in turn will affect the reputation of the business, reduce its sales and lower its goodwill.
2 Benefits: more efficient production because production is less reliant on staff; this leads to increased output, of better quality (new machines); lower costs elsewhere (fewer staff); technical economies of scale should occur.
  Drawbacks: staff morale will be affected as a result of some staff losing their jobs; retraining may be required, which will add to the firm's costs; work may become more routine, which may lower staff morale and lead to boredom; this could increase labour turnover.

SELLING THE PRODUCTS

Marketing in business

A

1 c 2 b 3 d 4 b 5 b

B

1 Tick d, f, h.
2 a) Market segmentation helps a business to target its market.
  b) When a firm concentrates on one market segment only, it is trading in a niche market. An example of such a business is *The Sock Shop*.
  c) A marketing department will link a firm's production to consumption.
3 The links are: a with iii; b with i; ii and v; c with iii and iv.

C

1 The 'market' is a place where goods and services are bought and sold. The market may be local (e.g. a village market), national (e.g. UK postage stamps) or international (e.g. cars).
2 a) It helps the company analyse sales and other trends; it allows advertising and sales promotion to be targeted at certain parts of the market; it enables products to be tailored to different types of customer.
  b) Price: a low price strategy due to competition and the buying power of the supermarkets.
  Place: distribution to supermarket depots, the frequency being set by the supermarket chain, and the positioning in the store also being set by the chain. Promotion: the ice cream must be promoted to supermarkets, not the general public, which means using (e.g.) trade magazines and direct selling. Product: market research will be needed to assess demand and the level of competition, and the company could work with supermarkets to get their ideas on packaging and labelling requirements.
3 Typical features are: individuals will pay themselves, business customers get the company to pay; individuals have full choice, business customers' choices may be restricted; individuals will be interested in cars only, business clients in cars and vans. As a result, the company might use local newspaper advertising to attract individuals, and use its existing customer database; for business customers it could sell direct through contacting local firms, or promote its special finance or leasing arrangements.

Market research

A

1 b 2 d 3 a 4 c 5 c

B

1 Tick b and c.
2 Market research: examining a market. Marketing research: examining all aspects of marketing (including market research).
3 a) no b) yes
  c) yes d) no

C

1 a) The role of market research for *Tesco* is to discover what its customers want. *Tesco* faces strong competition, e.g. from businesses such as *Sainsbury's*, *Asda* and *Morrisons*: as a result, it must supply its customers with what they want, or they may switch to buying from *Tesco's* competitors.
  b) The company will need to carry out market research, e.g. by checking with *Tesco* how successful its clothes are. It may sell these clothes in other markets, so market research will be necessary.
2 a) Sandra could find out about her local market through primary research (e.g. asking local people about their likes and dislikes), and secondary research (e.g. checking the size of the local population).
  b) i) Their buying habits such as how often they buy ornaments (e.g. birthday presents, Christmas); how often they visit the area where her shop is to be located (to check likely customer numbers).
  ii) Sandra could interview people on the street, asking them to complete a questionnaire; she could conduct a telephone survey, asking local people questions over the phone; she could research statistics, e.g. buying patterns and trends, the size of the local population.

Product

A

1 c 2 c 3 d 4 a 5 c

B

1

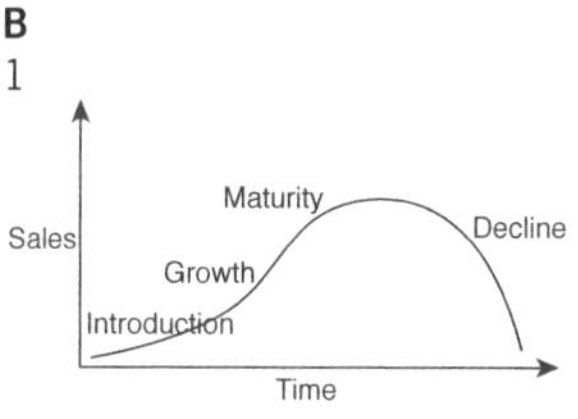

2 Link: Introduction with Problem Child; Growth with Star; Maturity with Cash Cow; and Decline with Dog.
3 Product items: a, c.

C

1 a) Branding helps the business market its product, e.g. by advertising the brand name. A brand name is a guarantee to customers that, when they next buy the same branded item, it will be virtually identical to the previous one bought. As a result, repeat purchases take place, and customer loyalty is established.
  Branding helps a business differentiate its products from those of its competitors.
  b) Brand names give products an identity: they also give companies an identity. A company that has a successful product can use this success to sell other products carrying its name. It uses successful brands to create a good business image, which will help it sell other goods and services. However, one

poor product may reduce the company's sales of its other products, because its image is affected.

2 a) By introducing new products, a company can respond to changing consumer tastes (e.g. a desire for new products) and changing market conditions (e.g. a competitor brings out a more advanced model).

b) Product differentiation allows branding to take place. Examples of products differentiated by brand names include clothes and tinned and bottled foodstuffs. Businesses achieve differentiation through (e.g.) creating a distinctive display or product design (e.g. certain car shapes such as the 'Beetle'), and making advertising fit a certain image (e.g. luxury chocolates).

Price

A

1 d 2 b 3 b 4 d 5 a

B

1 If the price of a product is not right, customers will buy products sold by competitors. Lost customers mean lost revenue for the business, and this in turn means lost profits.

2 a) cost-plus b) penetration c) penetration d) skimming e) skimming f) cost-plus

C

1 Room occupancy should increase, because lower prices make the hotel more competitive. However, it may lose its 'exclusive' image, which could affect its market position. Profits may increase: this will depend on whether the hotel can increase the number of visitors to compensate for a lower revenue from each room.

2 a) Penetration; skimming; cost-plus.

b) Skimming: this can be justified because the company has produced and used an expensive new non-stick coating. A high (skimming) price is possible because this is a unique product: the high price may allow the company to recover its costs before competitors enter the market and force its prices down.

c) Businesses in the private sector need to make profits for their owners, and need to be profitable (i.e. profit is measured against the investment used to make it). To be competitive, businesses have to control their prices, and low prices affect the level of profits being made. Pricing policy is therefore this 'balancing act'.

Place

A

1 d 2 c 3 a 4 c 5 b

B

1 a) Retailer → producer → wholesaler.

2 a) i b) ii

C

1 a) Manufacturer → retailer → consumer.

b) *Foodfare Ltd* receives feedback on its goods direct from the retailer, so it can take appropriate action quickly.

c) Costs of storage; costs of transport (e.g. petrol, maintenance); drivers' wages.

2 a) The company uses a broader approach to distribution, e.g. agents and wholesalers as well as direct to retailers.

b) The company is entering different markets, e.g. hotel chains, and as a result will need to use channels that are appropriate to these markets.

3 a) It is open 24 hours a day; reaches people outside her local area; inexpensive.

b) Setting up her site; getting her site known; arranging payment; arranging delivery.

Promoting by Advertising

A

1 d 2 a 3 c 4 c 5 d

B

1 Because television advertising is the most expensive form, the larger companies tend to use it. It creates great impact through its use of movement and sound. Alternative media such as newspapers allow readers to keep a copy of the advert because it is in a permanent form, unlike TV. Local radio is often used nowadays: it is less expensive than TV, but it has a smaller audience.

2 a) against b) for c) for d) for e) against

C

1 a) The people at whom the products are aimed: in this case, people who are interested in these old films.

b) Specialist magazines: these are inexpensive, and are aimed at people interested in these films. The cinema: people interested in modern films may also be interested in old films.

c) Different media are needed, since the media named in b) are aimed at the target audience for silent movies. The target audience for the blank CDs are retailers, so trade advertising and direct selling will be more appropriate.

2 a) Computer or internet magazines: these are aimed at people interested in computers and the internet.

b) It is not appropriate: the sale of glues and solvents is restricted to those aged over 18, and it is difficult to check ages on the internet; people interested in DIY would not use the internet to buy these products, since it is easier and more immediate to use high- street and out-of-town DIY shops.

Other types of promotion

A

1 a 2 d 3 b 4 a 5 b

B

1 The links are: a with iii; b with v; c with i; d with ii; e with iv; f with vi.

2 Correct order: c, b, d, a.

C

1 Leaflets through local people's doors, explaining about the opening. Competitions for those who attend the opening (e.g. to win free CDs and DVDs).

2 a) It is an industrial market, and many buyers expect a personal visit; the sales representative can explain technical and other features about the machinery face- to-face.

b) It is expensive: the company has to employ specialist sales staff, and meet travel and other costs.

3 Offering prizes: e.g. people attending the grand opening and taking a test drive are invited to enter a draw for a new car. Special offers: e.g. buy a new car in the first 3 months, and the company will pay the VAT on it. In both cases, sales will take place, and people will be encouraged to visit the new showroom.

4 a) It is promotion of the business, to improve the business's image.

b) The business is likely to have a PR officer, who will be responsible for promoting positive images of the business, e.g. by getting press releases printed in local papers.

ACKNOWLEDGEMENTS

The author and publisher are grateful to the copyright holders for permission to use quoted materials and photographs.

Every effort has been made to trace the copyright holders and to obtain their permission for the use of copyright material. The author and publisher will gladly receive information enabling them to rectify any error or omission in subsequent editions.

Letts Educational
4 Grosvenor Place
London SW1X 7DL

School enquiries: 015395 64910
Parent & student enquiries: 015395 64913
Email: mail@lettsed.co.uk
Website: www.letts-educational.com

First published 2007

British Library Cataloguing in Publication Data. A CIP record of this book is available from the British Library.

ISBN: 9781843157939

Letts Educational is a division of Huveaux plc.

Book concept and development: Helen Jacobs, Publishing Development Director

Editorial: Catherine Dakin and Rebecca Skinner
Author: David Floyd

Cover design: Angela English
Inside concept design: Starfish Design
Text design and layout: Ken Vail Graphic Design

C

These are GCSE-style questions. Answer all parts of the questions. Continue on a separate sheet where necessary.

1 **Explain the role of an industrial tribunal.**

....

....

....

.... (4 marks)

2 **Meena works at *Simcox Ltd*, a factory making metal parts for washing machines. She is a member of a trade union, and works as a shop steward. The union has carried out collective bargaining about pay levels, but this has broken down and the union is now in dispute with Meena's employer.**

a) Explain the terms underlined above.

Trade union: ....

Shop steward: ....

Collective bargaining: ....

In dispute: .... (4 marks)

b) Meena's trade union has balloted for an official strike over its pay dispute and members have voted to take strike action. Explain how this action, if it goes ahead, is likely to affect the following:

Employees such as Meena. ....

....

....

Meena's employers. ....

....

.... (8 marks)

c) Explain ways in which the Advisory, Conciliation and Arbitration Service (ACAS) might help resolve the dispute.

....

....

....

.... (4 marks)

Score /20

For more on this topic see pages 50–51 of your Success Guide.

Total score /35

How well did you do? ✗ 0–6 Try again 7–16 Getting there 17–26 Good work 27–35 Excellent! ✓

Finance for business

A

Choose just one answer: a, b, c or d.

1 Part of the profits made by a business might be used to:
a) revalue
b) reorder
c) regulate
d) reinvest **(1 mark)**

2 A lender providing a loan to a company might ask for:
a) security
b) liability
c) distribution
d) research **(1 mark)**

3 A long-term loan made to a company is a:
a) debenture b) dividend
c) debtor d) debit **(1 mark)**

4 Shares are most closely associated with businesses in the:
a) public sector
b) private sector
c) primary sector
d) professional sector **(1 mark)**

5 Selling a business debt is known as:
a) factoring
b) trading
c) granting
d) taxing **(1 mark)**

Score /5

B

Answer all parts of all questions.

1 Tick the correct box to classify each of the following as an internal or an external source of finance.

	Internal	External
a) A grant from the government	☐	☐
b) Sales that the business makes	☐	☐
c) Retained profits by the business	☐	☐
d) Selling the business debts	☐	☐
e) Borrowing from friends	☐	☐
f) Using 'trade credit'	☐	☐
g) Selling any surplus assets	☐	☐

(7 marks)

2 Delete the word or phrase that does not apply.
a) A public limited company can/cannot advertise its shares for sale to the general public.
b) Ordinary shares/Preference shares normally carry a vote. These shares receive interest/a dividend.
c) Debenture holders are lenders to/shareholders of a company. Debentures receive interest/a dividend.

(5 marks)

Score /12

C These are GCSE-style questions. Answer all parts of the questions. Continue on a separate sheet where necessary.

1 ***MM Ltd*** **is an expanding company in a growing sector of the economy.** ***MM Ltd*** **wants to use its retained profits to finance its expansion, rather than take out a loan from a bank. Explain the advantages and disadvantages of this policy.**

....

....

.... **(6 marks)**

2 **Arthur and Brian are in partnership, growing vegetables on their farm. They use Chen's transport company to get their produce to a chain of greengrocer shops owned by Diane. Arthur and Brian need finance to employ more seasonal staff; Chen needs finance to buy a new lorry; and Diane needs finance to redecorate one of her shops.**

a) Identify one appropriate external source of finance for each of these businesses. Choose a different source in each case and justify each choice.

....

....

.... **(6 marks)**

b) Explain the reasons why each business is likely to use different sources of finance.

....

.... **(4 marks)**

3 ***PDG Ltd*** **needs to borrow in order to buy the stock it needs to sell.**

a) Describe two ways that a bank might help *PDG Ltd.*

....

.... **(4 marks)**

b) Explain whether using trade credit might help *PDG Ltd* in this situation.

....

.... **(4 marks)**

Score /24

For more on this topic see pages 54–55 of your Success Guide. Total score /41

How well did you do? 0–8 Try again 9–20 Getting there 21–34 Good work 35–41 Excellent!

Financial records in business 1

A

Choose just one answer: a, b, c or d.

1 The difference between a business's income and its costs is its:
a) price b) piece-rate
c) premium d) profit **(1 mark)**

2 People who sell goods on credit to a business are known as:
a) debtors b) creditors
c) owners d) shareholders **(1 mark)**

3 Records of customers buying goods on credit are held in the:
a) purchases ledger b) general ledger
c) sales ledger d) cash book **(1 mark)**

4 Vehicles owned by a business are:
a) assets
b) liabilities
c) expenses
d) revenues **(1 mark)**

5 Machinery goes down in value each year. This is known as:
a) devaluation
b) dismissal
c) depreciation
d) delegation **(1 mark)**

Score /5

B

Answer all parts of all questions.

1 Complete the following sentences using the words from the box below.

A trading profit and loss account contains information on ....,
...., ... and .... profit.

A balance sheet shows details of a business's ....,
.... and ....

liabilities	revenues	gross	expenses	net	assets	capital

(7 marks)

2 An inexperienced accounts clerk has constructed the account below. It contains a number of errors, which mean that the wrong net profit figure is shown. Construct a correct account and calculate the net profit.

Trading, profit and loss account

	(£000)	(£000)
Sales		755
Interest paid		45
		800
Other income	25	
Cost of goods sold	100	
Salaries	240	
Rent and rates	60	
Interest received	5	
Other expenses	70	
		500
Net profit		300

(6 marks)

Score /13

C

This is a GCSE-style question. Answer all parts of the question. Continue on a separate sheet where necessary.

1 Extracts from the financial statements of *GoodSounds Ltd*, a company making radios, are given below:

	£ 000
Capital and reserves	2 000
Current assets	1 500
Current liabilities	1 000
Fixed assets	4 000
Long-term liabilities	2 500
Net sales	2 400
Total expenses	1 500

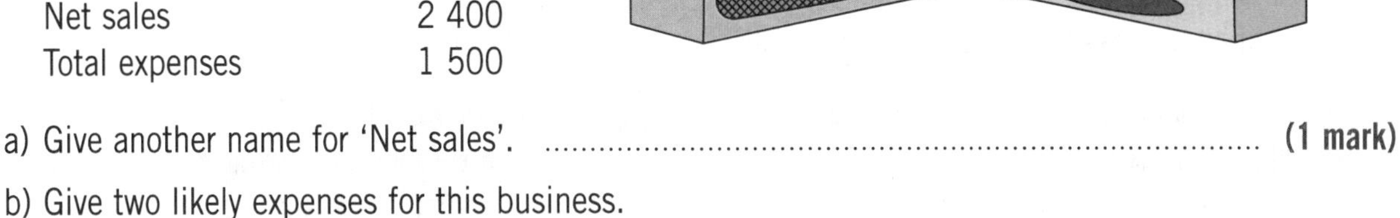

a) Give another name for 'Net sales'. .... **(1 mark)**

b) Give two likely expenses for this business.

.... **(2 marks)**

c) Identify under which of the headings in the financial statement above these items will appear.

i) The debtors of *GoodSounds Ltd*: ....

ii) *GoodSounds Ltd*'s creditors: ....

iii) The closing stock of raw materials for *GoodSounds Ltd*: ....

iv) A 5-year loan from *GoodSounds Ltd*'s bank: ....

v) Money invested in *GoodSounds Ltd* by its shareholders: .... **(5 marks)**

d) Calculate the profit made by *GoodSounds Ltd* as shown by these items.

.... **(2 marks)**

e) In the box below, construct a balance sheet from the items listed.

(4 marks)

f) i) Calculate the working capital for *GoodSounds Ltd*.

.... **(2 marks)**

ii) Explain the problems that the directors of *GoodSounds Ltd* might face if the company became short of working capital.

....

.... **(4 marks)**

Score /20

For more on this topic see pages 56–57 of your Success Guide. Total score /38

How well did you do? 0–9 Try again 10–19 Getting there 20–29 Good work 30–38 Excellent!

Financial records in business 2

A

Choose just one answer: a, b, c or d.

1 A firm makes a loss when:
a) revenue is less than costs
b) costs are less than revenue
c) assets are less than liabilities
d) liabilities are less than assets (1 mark)

2 Records of suppliers selling goods on credit to a business are in its:
a) purchases ledger b) sales ledger
c) cash book d) general ledger (1 mark)

3 Gross profit is calculated in the firm's:
a) trading account
b) profit and loss account
c) balance sheet
d) cash budget (1 mark)

4 Liabilities are what a business:
a) owns
b) owes
c) rents
d) trades (1 mark)

5 A directors' report explains:
a) a sole trader's borrowing requirements
b) a partnership's assets and liabilities
c) a franchisee's net profit
d) a company's performance (1 mark)

Score /5

B

Answer all parts of all questions.

1 Classify each of the following as either an asset, a liability, an expense or revenue (an income).

a) Advertising costs asset/liability/expense/revenue
b) A bank loan asset/liability/expense/revenue
c) Capital from the owner asset/liability/expense/revenue
d) A debtor asset/liability/expense/revenue
e) The firm's sales asset/liability/expense/revenue
f) Salaries paid asset/liability/expense/revenue (6 marks)

2 Complete the missing words in the following sentences:

It is the role of financial accounting to c.. financial information from o.. documents such as invoices. This information is r.. in the accounts, and it can then be a.. by the accountant. The accountant will then c.. this information to other managers.

(5 marks)

Score /11

C This is a GCSE-style question. Answer all parts of the question. Continue on a separate sheet where necessary.

1 Study the following accounts and answer the questions that follow.

Dave's Cake Shop

Final accounts for the year ended 31 December

	£	£
Sales income		57 500
Less food costs	10 000	
Less drink costs	6 250	A
Gross profit		B
Expenses:		
Salaries	8 000	
Power	1 250	
Rent and rates	6 000	
Advertising	1 250	
Other costs	750	C
Net profit		D

a) Calculate and insert the missing figures at points A, B, C and D. **(4 marks)**

b) Explain why Dave is likely to be more interested in his net profit figure than in his gross profit figure.

....

.... **(6 marks)**

c) i) Identify two types of accounts that are not shown in the above account.

.... **(2 marks)**

ii) For each type of account, give two examples you might expect Dave's cake shop to have.

.... **(2 marks)**

iii) Name the final account in which these accounts will appear at the end of each year.

.... **(1 mark)**

d) Dave is not very happy with the amount of profit he is making. He has two plans: to stop employing a part-time assistant at weekends, or to stop advertising.

Explain one drawback of each plan that Dave needs to consider.

Stop employing part-time help: ....

....

Stop advertising: ....

.... **(6 marks)**

Score /21

For more on this topic see pages 56–57 of your Success Guide. Total score /37

How well did you do? ✗ 0–7 Try again 8–17 Getting there 18–29 Good work 30–37 Excellent! ✓

Interpreting business accounts 1

A

Choose just one answer: a, b, c or d.

1 Sales of £30 000 and gross profit of £6000 give a gross profit ratio of:

a) 6% b) 500%
c) 20% d) 24% (1 mark)

2 The different groups interested in a firm's financial performance are its:

a) shareholders
b) stakeholders
c) sponsors
d) stockbrokers (1 mark)

3 'ROCE' stands for:

a) return on creditors' earnings
b) return of customers' exports
c) return of corporate executive
d) return on capital employed (1 mark)

4 A firm's current ratio is calculated by comparing:

a) current assets to current liabilities
b) current assets less stock, to current liabilities
c) current assets to total liabilities
d) total assets to total liabilities (1 mark)

5 A firm's liquidity shows:

a) its profit levels
b) the amount of sales it makes
c) how much VAT and tax it pays
d) its ability to pay its debts (1 mark)

Score /5

B

Answer all parts of the question.

1 Fill in the missing values to complete these accounts.

	£000	£000
Sales		750
Opening stock	25	
Add purchases	425	
	☐	
Less closing stock	30	
Cost of sales		☐
Gross profit		☐
Rent and rates	40	
Selling expenses	10	
Office expenses	30	
Wages and salaries	20	
Total expenses		☐
Net profit		☐

Score /5

C

These are GCSE-style questions. Answer all parts of the questions. Continue on a separate sheet where necessary.

1 The following information comes from a company's final accounts.

	Year 1 (£000)	Year 2 (£000)	Year 3 (£000)
Sales	350	400	450
Gross profit	140	152	162
Net profit	56	48	36

a) Calculate the net profit margin for each year.

....

.... **(3 marks)**

b) Suggest two reasons for the change in the net profit margin from Year 1 to Year 3.

....

.... **(4 marks)**

2 The following extracts are from the accounts of *Car Clinic Ltd*, a garage that sells and services vehicles.

	This year £000	Last year £000
Sales	600	500
Purchases	360	325
Gross profit	240	175
Net profit	90	40
Stocks	100	100
Other current assets	100	150
Current liabilities	250	250
Capital employed	450	400

Calculate appropriate profitability and liquidity ratios, and comment on the financial position of *Car Clinic Ltd*.

....

....

....

....

....

....

....

....

.... **(12 marks)**

Score /19

For more on this topic see pages 58–59 of your Success Guide.

Total score /29

How well did you do? ✗ 0–7 Try again 8–14 Getting there 15-22 Good work 23–29 Excellent! ✓

Interpreting business accounts 2

A

Choose just one answer: a, b, c or d.

1 The net profit margin of a firm with £500 000 turnover and £50 000 net profit is:

a) 50% b) 1 000%
c) 10% d) 1% **(1 mark)**

2 Working capital is the difference between:

a) assets and liabilities
b) current assets and current liabilities
c) fixed assets and long-term liabilities
d) profit and loss **(1 mark)**

3 Banks and other lenders to a business are likely to be most interested in its:

a) liquidity
b) vehicles
c) competitors
d) stock **(1 mark)**

4 Creditors' collection period tells a firm:

a) how long its customers take to pay
b) how long it is taking to pay suppliers
c) how large its credit bills are
d) the credit terms it is offering **(1 mark)**

5 Ratios should be used to:

a) see the amount of profit being made
b) check how much tax needs paying
c) study financial trends
d) make sure that a balance sheet balances **(1 mark)**

Score /5

B

Answer all parts of all questions.

1 Match each stakeholder group with its appropriate interest.

Stakeholder	**Interest**
a) Employees	i) How likely that any borrowing can be repaid
b) Lenders	ii) How much tax is owed
c) Government	iii) How profitable the investment is likely to be
d) Shareholders	iv) How safe jobs are

(4 marks)

2 For each of the stakeholder groups, suggest one appropriate financial ratio that will be of interest to them.

a) Employees Ratio: ....
b) Lenders Ratio: ....
c) Government Ratio: ....
d) Shareholders Ratio: .... **(4 marks)**

3 Are these formulae right or wrong?

a) Debtors' collection period = $\frac{\text{debtors}}{\text{sales}} \times 365$

b) Gross profit margin = $\frac{\text{gross profit}}{\text{sales}} \times 365$ **(2 marks)**

Score /10

C This is a GCSE-style question. Answer all parts of the question. Continue on a separate sheet where necessary.

1 **The final accounts for two businesses of similar size and in the same industry are shown below.**

	Laurel Ltd £000	Hardy Ltd £000
Sales	750	600
Cost of sales	450	390
Gross profit	300	210
Expenses	150	120
Net profit	150	90
Fixed assets	400	500
Current assets	120	150
Current liabilities	160	100
Long-term liabilities	60	300
Capital and reserves	300	250
Details of current assets:		
Stocks	40	50
Debtors	60	50
Bank	20	50
Details of current liabilities:		
Creditors	75	50
Short-term borrowing	85	50

a) Calculate the following ratios for each company:

i) gross profit %: ....

ii) net profit %: ....

iii) return on capital employed: ....

iv) current ratio: ....

v) acid test: ....

vi) debtors' collection period: ....

vii) creditors' collection period: ....

viii) rate of stock turnover: .... **(16 marks)**

b) Compare the performance of these businesses as shown by the above ratios.

....

....

....

....

.... **(12 marks)**

Score /28

For more on this topic see pages 58–59 of your Success Guide. **Total score /43**

How well did you do? 0–8 Try again 9–20 Getting there 21–33 Good work 34–43 Excellent!

Costs in business

A

Choose just one answer: a, b, c or d.

1 Raw materials used to make a firm's products are:
a) fixed costs
b) variable costs
c) semi-fixed costs
d) semi-variable costs (1 mark)

2 Rent paid for business premises is a:
a) fixed cost
b) variable cost
c) semi-fixed cost
d) semi-variable cost (1 mark)

3 A standard cost is the cost that a good or service:
a) is
b) should be
c) will be
d) cannot be (1 mark)

4 Variable costs will change according to the number:
a) made
b) sold
c) stored
d) rented (1 mark)

5 'Overheads' are:
a) direct costs
b) indirect costs
c) fixed costs
d) variable costs (1 mark)

Score /5

B

Answer all parts of all questions.

1 *Car Clinic Ltd* sells and repairs vehicles. Classify these costs for *Car Clinic Ltd* by ticking the most appropriate box.

	a) Fixed	Variable	Semi-variable	b) Direct	Indirect
i) Office salaries	☐	☐	☐	☐	☐
ii) Oil used for car services	☐	☐	☐	☐	☐
iii) Mechanics' piece-work wages	☐	☐	☐	☐	☐
iv) Garage premises rates	☐	☐	☐	☐	☐
v) Depreciation of welding machine	☐	☐	☐	☐	☐
vi) Electricity bill	☐	☐	☐	☐	☐

(12 marks)

2 Are the following statements true or false?

	True	False
a) A semi-variable cost is also known as a semi-fixed cost.	☐	☐
b) The difference between the actual cost and the standard cost is called a variable.	☐	☐
c) An opportunity cost is the cost of not being able to do something else.	☐	☐
d) Fixed costs are also direct costs.	☐	☐
e) Direct costs plus indirect costs equal total costs.	☐	☐

(5 marks)

Score /17

C

These are GCSE-style questions. Answer all parts of the questions. Continue on a separate sheet where necessary.

1 ***Moorow Ltd* makes electrical goods, which it sells to the general public. The company has shops in the major towns and cities of the UK.**

a) Give two examples of fixed costs and two examples of variable costs for this business.

....

.... **(4 marks)**

b) Give two examples of direct costs and two examples of indirect costs for this business.

....

.... **(4 marks)**

c) Explain why it is important for the managers of *Moorow Ltd* to be able to classify their costs as:

i) fixed and variable

....

.... **(4 marks)**

ii) direct and indirect.

....

.... **(4 marks)**

2 ***Deltar Ltd* is a large manufacturing business that makes engine parts for cars.**

a) Explain how a standard costing system might be of use to *Deltar Ltd*.

....

.... **(3 marks)**

Both *Ford* and *Vauxhall* have approached the managers of *Deltar Ltd* to make a new engine part. The company cannot make parts for both of these car manufacturers.

b) Explain how the decision the managers must make is an example of an opportunity cost.

....

....

.... **(3 marks)**

Score /22

For more on this topic see pages 60–61 of your Success Guide.

Total score /44

How well did you do? 0–8 Try again 9–20 Getting there 21–34 Good work 35–44 Excellent!

Breaking even in business

A

Choose just one answer: a, b, c or d.

1 The point at which a business goes from loss into profit can be seen on:
a) a pie chart
b) a break-even chart
c) a bar chart
d) an organisation chart (1 mark)

2 A fixed cost is one that:
a) does change as output changes
b) does not change as output changes
c) does change as profit changes
d) does not change as profit changes (1 mark)

3 Contribution in break-even analysis is the difference between:
a) fixed costs and variable costs
b) fixed costs and sales
c) sales and variable costs
d) profit and loss (1 mark)

4 The difference between the break-even output level and the expected output is the:
a) margin of safety
b) area of loss
c) total fixed costs
d) break-even revenue (1 mark)

5 Total costs in break-even analysis are shown by:
a) fixed costs plus direct costs
b) fixed costs plus variable costs
c) sales less fixed costs
d) sales less variable costs (1 mark)

Score /5

B

Answer all parts of all questions.

1 Calculate the break-even point (units and revenue) in the following situations.

	Selling price (£)	Variable cost per unit (£)	Total fixed costs (£)	Break-even units	Break-even revenue (£)
a)	20	8	30000		
b)	44	32	24480		
c)	12.50	5.50	21350		

(6 marks)

2 Correct any errors or omissions on the following break-even chart.

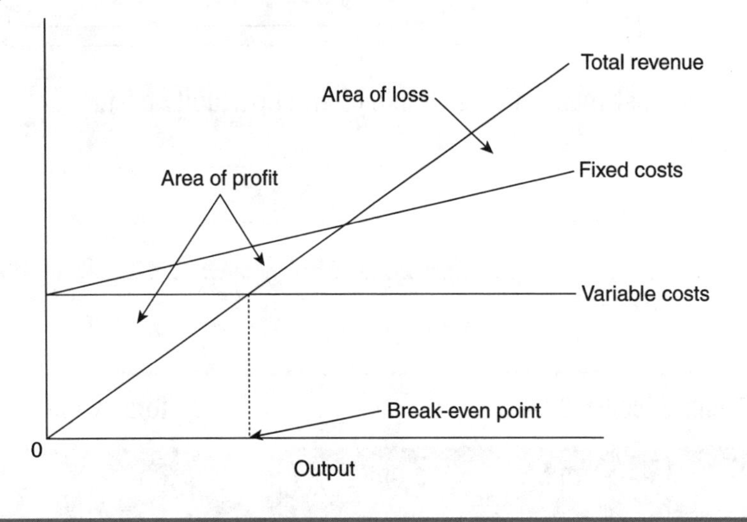

(6 marks)

Score /12

C

These are GCSE-style questions. Answer all parts of the questions. Continue on a separate sheet where necessary.

1 The table below contains sales and costs for a business's Internet Sales department. Complete the empty boxes in the table and use your results to state the break-even point.

Number sold	Fixed costs (£)	Variable costs (£)	Total costs (£)	Sales revenue (£)
0	200000	0	200000	0
1000	200000	20000	220000	60000
2000	200000			
3000	200000			
4000	200000			
5000	200000			
6000	200000			

Break-even point (units): .... **(4 marks)**

2 Construct a suitably labelled and titled break-even chart on the graph paper below using the following information.

JK Ltd makes sports shoes. It expects to sell 7500 pairs in this trading period at an average price of £25 per pair.
The shoes are made from:

- leather, costing £6 per pair of shoes
- laces, which cost 50p for each shoe
- polish and other materials, costing £1 per pair.

JK Ltd's other costs for this period are:

- wages, paid at £7 for each pair of shoes made
- office salaries, totalling £50 000
- rent, rates and other fixed costs, which total £5000.

Break-even point (units):

....

....

Break-even point (revenue):

....

....

Margin of safety (units):

....

....

(15 marks)

For more on this topic see pages 62–63 of your Success Guide.

Total score /36

How well did you do? 0–7 Try again 8–17 Getting there 18–29 Good work 30–36 Excellent!

Budgeting in business

A

Choose just one answer: a, b, c or d.

1 A company normally uses a cash budget to help it:
a) appraise its staff
b) merge with another business
c) forecast money movements
d) sell its products (1 mark)

2 Budget preparation is controlled by the budget:
a) consumer
b) committee
c) creditor
d) company (1 mark)

3 A budget is best defined as:
a) a financial gain
b) a financial debt
c) a financial loss
d) a financial plan (1 mark)

4 A sales budget shows a firm's expected:
a) turnover
b) production
c) cash
d) capital expenditure (1 mark)

5 Staff who meet their budget targets are likely to be:
a) annoyed
b) dismissed
c) transferred
d) motivated (1 mark)

Score /5

B

Answer all parts of all questions.

1 Tick the correct box to classify each of the following as a source or a use of cash for a firm.

	Source	Use
a) Buying a new computer	☐	☐
b) Money received from selling products	☐	☐
c) An overdraft from the bank	☐	☐
d) Money invested by the owner	☐	☐
e) Selling an old vehicle the firm owns	☐	☐
f) Paying the electricity bill	☐	☐
g) Paying VAT owing to the government	☐	☐

(7 marks)

2 *NGH plc* is a large manufacturing company that makes parts for cars and other vehicles. Its departments include Production, Marketing, Purchasing and Accounts.

Name three budgets that *NGH plc* is likely to set.

....

....

.... (3 marks)

Score /10

C

These are GCSE-style questions. Answer all parts of the questions. Continue on a separate sheet where necessary.

1 ***Droflet United*** **is a football club. Its team is made up of part-time players who also have other jobs. The number of supporters who pay to watch the team varies depending on the team's results. The manager is given a budget for players' wages and he must keep within it.**

Explain the likely reasons why the directors of *Droflet United* set a budget for the manager.

.... **(4 marks)**

2 **Here is a cash flow forecast prepared for a company.**

a) Complete the figures missing from the shaded boxes.

Cash flow forecast for 6 months, January – June (£000)						
	Jan	**Feb**	**Mar**	**Apr**	**May**	**Jun**
Opening Balance	25		11		52	50
Receipts:						
Cash from sales	120	120	120	130	120	
Sale of asset				45		
Payments:						
Staff salaries	45	45	45	46	46	46
Material purchases	60	62	62	60	58	58
Purchase of assets	15		15			20
Other payments	11	16	12	14	18	15
Closing balance	14	11		52	50	21

(4 marks)

b) Explain the action this company is likely to take as a result of this forecast:

i) At the end of March: .... **(2 marks)**

ii) During most of April and May: .... **(2 marks)**

3 **The summary to the right shows the actual cash flow for a business against its budgeted cash flow for a month's trading.**

Outflow (expenditure)			**Inflow (receipts)**		
	Forecast (£)	**Actual (£)**		**Forecast (£)**	**Actual (£)**
Pay	4500	4800	Cash sales	10000	11000
Materials	3500	2800	Payments from credit customers	8000	7500
Office costs	8000	8000			
	16000	**15600**		**18000**	**18500**

a) Define the term 'net cash flow'.

.... **(2 marks)**

b) i) Calculate the difference between the actual and the budgeted net cash flows for this business.

.... **(1 mark)**

ii) Analyse four reasons for the difference between the actual and budgeted net cash flows.

....

.... **(4 marks)**

Score /19

For more on this topic see pages 64–65 of your Success Guide.

Total score /34

How well did you do? ✗ 0–6 Try again 7–16 Getting there 17–27 Good work 28–34 Excellent! ✓

Production in business

A

Choose just one answer: a, b, c or d.

1 Job and batch are methods of:
a) finance b) marketing
c) production d) purchasing **(1 mark)**

2 Flow-line production is also known as:
a) one-off production
b) mass production
c) chain of production
d) just-in-time production **(1 mark)**

3 'Kaizen' means:
a) long-term production targets
b) the science of using robots in production
c) continuous improvement
d) efficiency in turning inputs into outputs
(1 mark)

4 Items made to a customer's requirements use:
a) job production
b) batch production
c) continuous production
d) flow-line production **(1 mark)**

5 'Just-in-time' stockholding seeks to:
a) increase the number of stock items held
b) increase the variety of stock items held
c) cut the costs of holding stock
d) cut the number of machines that use stock
(1 mark)

Score /5

B

Answer all parts of all questions.

1 Match the example to the most likely method of production used (job, batch or mass).

Example	Method of production
a) A tin of paint bought from a major DIY store	....
b) A large holiday cruise ship	....
c) An order of 120 identical mobile phone cases	....
d) A jar of jam sold in a large grocery chain	....
e) A Ford car	....
f) A house built to order	....
g) 20 fuchsias (garden plants) grown to order	.... **(7 marks)**

2 Delete the incorrect word or phrase in the following sentences.

Mass production, also known as continuous production/complete production, is normally associated with automation. As a result, machinery replaces people/people replace machinery. Total costs are increased/reduced but staff who work in a largely automated factory often become bored/are highly motivated. Mass production depends on the product having a very high demand/very low demand.

(5 marks)

Score /12

C

These are GCSE-style questions. Answer all parts of the questions. Continue on a separate sheet where necessary.

1 ***Memories Ltd*** **deals in film and music souvenirs. Some of these items, such as clothes worn in films, are hand-made and are sold to collectors. Other items are made for sale in shops throughout the UK.**

a) Name the most appropriate method of production for the following:

i) The collectors' market items

....

ii) The shop items

.... **(2 marks)**

b) The items sold to collectors are far more expensive to make than the shop items. Explain three reasons for this.

....

....

.... **(6 marks)**

2 **At a recent board meeting of *Boxit Ltd*, a large manufacturer of cartons and boxes, the Production Director said: 'It is important that we produce our products using modern methods, in a simple and well-organised way.'**

a) Explain the likely production method used by *Boxit Ltd*.

.... **(2 marks)**

b) Outline two advantages to *Boxit Ltd* of using this production method.

....

.... **(2 marks)**

c) Explain two disadvantages to the staff of *Boxit Ltd* who are employed in the Production department making cartons and boxes.

....

.... **(4 marks)**

d) Explain how a system of 'just-in-time' stockholding is likely to affect the work of the Production department at *Boxit Ltd*.

....

.... **(4 marks)**

Score /20

For more on this topic see pages 68–69 of your Success Guide.

Total score /37

How well did you do? 0–7 Try again 8–18 Getting there 19–29 Good work 30–37 Excellent!

Economies of scale

A

Choose just one answer: a, b, c or d.

1 Bulk buying is an example of a:
a) marketing economy
b) purchasing economy
c) managerial economy
d) risk-bearing economy **(1 mark)**

2 A financial economy of scale comes from receiving a loan at a:
a) lower interest rate
b) zero interest rate
c) higher interest rate
d) negative interest rate **(1 mark)**

3 When all businesses in an industry benefit, this is known as:
a) an internal economy of scale
b) an external economy of scale
c) a diseconomy of scale
d) an economic economy of scale **(1 mark)**

4 Diseconomies of scale start to occur when unit costs:
a) rise
b) fall
c) rise and fall
d) stay the same **(1 mark)**

5 When larger firms 'diversify', they spread their risk by:
a) not relying on only one product or market
b) producing their products more quickly
c) refusing to sell in risky markets
d) selling fewer products than they did before **(1 mark)**

Score /5

B

Answer all parts of all questions.

1 Complete the 'Economy of scale' column, matching the examples to the correct economies.

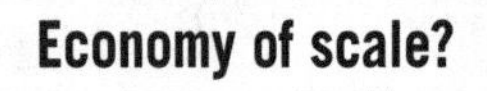

Example	Economy of scale?
a) Lower advertising costs per unit	....
b) Using more advanced machinery	....
c) Negotiating lower raw material prices	....
d) Negotiating a lower overdraft interest rate	....
e) Employing a specialist ICT manager	....

(5 marks)

2 Delete the incorrect word or phrase in the following sentences.

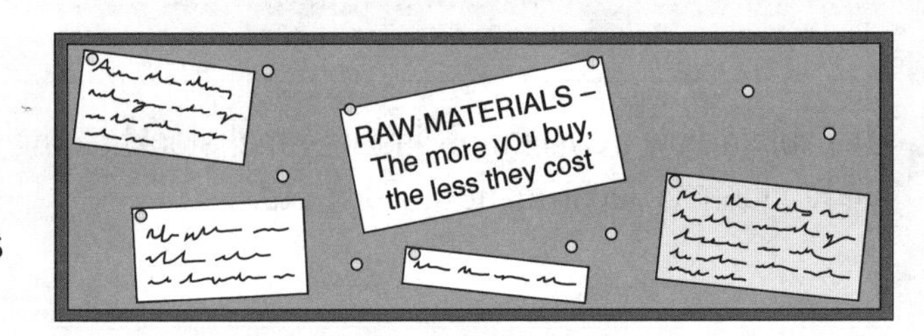

A firm's costs can be classed as either fixed or variable. As its output increases, the firm's fixed costs will increase in line with output/still stay at the same level. As a result, although total costs are still increasing/falling, the average cost for each product made is rising/falling. The cost per unit made is therefore higher/lower. This is because the firm's fixed costs are greater than its variable costs/being spread over a larger output.

(5 marks)

Score /10

C

These are GCSE-style questions. Answer all parts of the questions. Continue on a separate sheet where necessary.

1 ***PoshPots Ltd*** **is a company that makes pottery items. Its products include mass-produced china cups, saucers and plates, and hand-made vases and other decorative pots. The company is located in Stoke-on-Trent, in an area known as 'The Potteries'. This area is famous for the quality of pottery made, although many firms in the area have closed down due to overseas competition.**

a) Explain the benefits that *PoshPots Ltd* is likely to gain from being based in 'The Potteries'.

....

....

.... **(6 marks)**

b) i) Outline the likely economies of scale that *PoshPots Ltd* will gain from mass producing its china.

....

.... **(4 marks)**

ii) Explain why *PoshPots Ltd* is less likely to benefit from economies of scale when making the vases and other decorative pots.

....

.... **(4 marks)**

2 ***Sound Goods Ltd*** **is a business that makes hi-fi and stereo equipment. The company has a tall hierarchy and communication between the levels is slow.** ***Sound Goods Ltd*** **has recently experienced some diseconomies of scale.**

a) Define the term 'diseconomies of scale'.

.... **(2 marks)**

b) Explain the likely effect that slow communication will have on the following:

i) The managers of *Sound Goods Ltd*

.... **(3 marks)**

ii) The employees of *Sound Goods Ltd*

.... **(3 marks)**

c) Outline appropriate strategies that the managers of *Sound Goods Ltd* might take in order to prevent the effects of diseconomies of scale.

....

....

.... **(6 marks)**

Score /28

For more on this topic see pages 70–71 of your Success Guide.

Total score /43

How well did you do? ✗ 0–8 Try again 9–20 Getting there 21–34 Good work 35–43 Excellent! ✓

Productivity

A

Choose just one answer: a, b, c or d.

1 A business using all its resources:
a) has surplus capacity
b) is working at full capacity
c) must be using mass production methods
d) has highly motivated staff **(1 mark)**

2 'Substituting capital for labour' takes place when a business:
a) replaces old staff with younger staff
b) replaces staff with equipment
c) replaces old equipment with new equipment
d) replaces equipment with staff **(1 mark)**

3 One of the four factors of production is:
a) money b) vehicles
c) stock d) land **(1 mark)**

4 'CAD' stands for:
a) creditors and debtors
b) current asset dividend
c) computer-aided design
d) calculating average discount **(1 mark)**

5 Productivity measures:
a) outputs against inputs
b) costs against revenues
c) capital against labour
d) number made against number sold **(1 mark)**

Score /5

B

Answer all parts of all questions.

1 Match the statement with its correct description.

Statement	Description
a) The four factors of production	i) Output measured against inputs used
b) Capital intensity	ii) The use of robots
c) Production	iii) Land, labour, capital, enterprise
d) Surplus capacity	iv) How much a firm depends on machines and equipment
e) Productivity	v) Unused resources
f) CAM	vi) The output of a business

(6 marks)

2 Select the correct alternative to complete the following sentences.

a) One way to improve a firm's productivity is to use the same:
  i) inputs more efficiently to produce higher output.
  ii) outputs more efficiently to produce higher input.

b) Another way to improve productivity is to produce the same:
  i) input with less output.
  ii) output with less input. **(2 marks)**

Score /8

C

These are GCSE-style questions. Answer all parts of the questions. Continue on a separate sheet where necessary.

1 ***BrightLight plc*** **produces torches, lamps and light bulbs in factories in two nearby towns. One factory was built early in the 20th century and has an old-fashioned layout. The other factory is a much more recent building, housing modern equipment in a modern layout.**

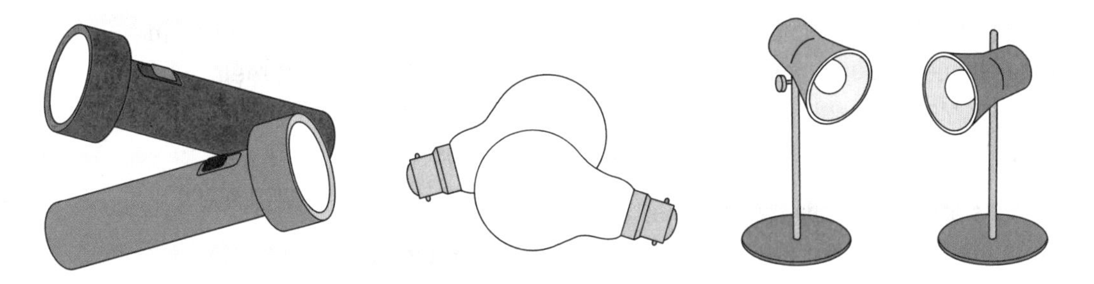

BrightLight plc **operates in a highly competitive market and needs to keep its costs under close control. It is currently operating well below full capacity, with some full-time staff working well below full-time hours. The directors are considering closing and selling the old factory. They are asking staff who work there, and who still want to work for the company, to travel to the new factory, which is 20 miles away.**

Explain why productivity is important to ***BrightLight plc***

....

.... **(4 marks)**

2 a) Outline how the proposed action of the directors will reduce surplus capacity at *BrightLight plc.*

....

.... **(2 marks)**

b) Explain how this action, when carried out, is likely to improve productivity.

....

.... **(4 marks)**

c) Describe three likely problems that the proposed action of the directors is likely to create for *BrightLight plc.*

....

....

.... **(6 marks)**

The directors' proposals have been carried out and productive capacity at ***BrightLight plc*** **has improved.**

d) Explain two likely problems if *BrightLight plc* is now working at or near full capacity.

....

.... **(4 marks)**

Score /20

For more on this topic see pages 72–73 of your Success Guide.

Total score /33

How well did you do? 0–6 Try again 7–16 Getting there 17–25 Good work 26–33 Excellent!

Quality and stock control

A

Choose just one answer: a, b, c or d.

1 'TQM' stands for:
a) Trade Quotation Management
b) Travelling Queue Management
c) Total Quality Management
d) Target Quota Management **(1 mark)**

2 Pens, paperclips and memo pads are examples of:
a) raw materials stock
b) work in progress stock
c) production stock
d) administrative stock **(1 mark)**

3 A key feature of quality control is:
a) setting quality standards
b) checking that quality standards are being kept
c) offering after-sales service and guarantees
d) setting high stock levels **(1 mark)**

4 The optimum stock level:
a) keeps costs to a minimum
b) keeps stocks at their maximum level
c) is the amount of stock that should be ordered
d) is the undamaged stock **(1 mark)**

5 Total Quality Management seeks to:
a) get it right first time
b) get it right last time
c) get it right next time
d) never get it right **(1 mark)**

Score /5

B

Answer all parts of all questions.

1 Indicate whether the stock-holding problem is due to too much or too little stock.

a) Increased storage expenses — too much stock/too little stock
b) Working capital is 'tied up' — too much stock/too little stock
c) Lost production in the factory — too much stock/too little stock
d) Customers' orders are not being met — too much stock/too little stock
e) There is a greater risk of theft — too much stock/too little stock
f) Production staff are paid for 'idle time' — too much stock/too little stock **(6 marks)**

2 Match each stock level with the correct definition.

a) Maximum stock — i) The level below which stock should not fall
b) Minimum stock — ii) The level at which a new order is made
c) Reorder level — iii) The highest level of stock
d) Reorder quantity — iv) The number of stock items to be delivered **(4 marks)**

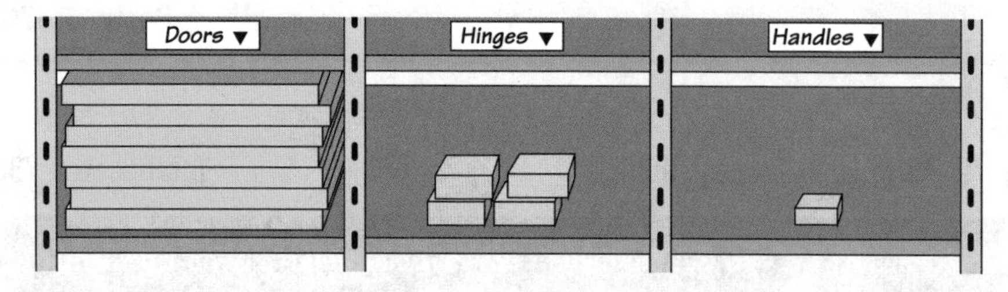

Score /10

C

These are GCSE-style questions. Answer all parts of the questions. Continue on a separate sheet where necessary.

1 ***TastyFoods Ltd*** **makes fresh sandwiches and snacks. Although staff are careful when ordering bread and foodstuffs for the sandwiches and snacks, there is still a lot of waste due to ordering and holding too much.**

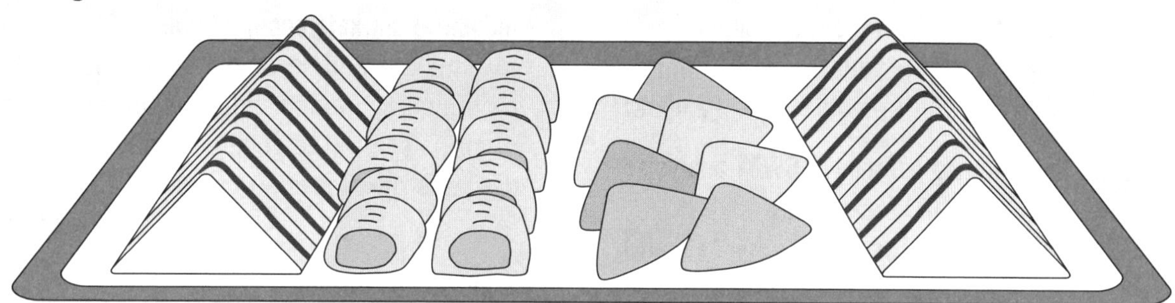

TastyFoods Ltd **is supplied by a local bakery, which at the moment makes a single delivery each day, and by a local greengrocer store that supplies salad and other sandwich fillings.**

a) The managers of *TastyFoods Ltd* want to operate a 'just-in-time' stock system. Describe how this system would affect the work of *TastyFoods Ltd.*

....

....

.... **(4 marks)**

b) Suggest two advantages that this system might bring to *TastyFoods Ltd.*

....

.... **(4 marks)**

c) Explain why a TQM system is likely to be appropriate for *TastyFoods Ltd.*

....

....

....

.... **(8 marks)**

2 ***Safe Electrics Ltd*** **manufactures light fittings. It has recently installed technically advanced machinery on its production lines. This machinery is controlled by computers and replaces old machines. Fewer staff will now be needed.**

Examine the likely benefits and drawbacks to ***Safe Electrics Ltd*** **of replacing its machinery.**

Benefits: ....

....

Drawbacks: ....

.... **(8 marks)**

Score /24

For more on this topic see pages 74–75 of your Success Guide.

Total score /39

How well did you do? 0–8 Try again 9–19 Getting there 20–31 Good work 32–39 Excellent!

Marketing in business

A

Choose just one answer: a, b, c or d.

1 In the marketing mix, the 'P' for distribution is:
a) price b) product
c) place d) promotion **(1 mark)**

2 Which of the following is found in SWOT analysis?
a) Sales b) Weaknesses
c) Objectives d) Turnover **(1 mark)**

3 Market segmentation involves:
a) calculating the market share held by a business
b) gathering primary and secondary data about a product
c) carrying out marketing through the 'four Ps'
d) splitting a market into its different parts
(1 mark)

4 Industrial markets occur where:
a) all goods and services are bought and sold
b) firms buy items used in business
c) firms sell to the general public
d) industrial stocks and shares are sold
(1 mark)

5 'USP' stands for:
a) Under-Stated Price
b) Unique Selling Point
c) Unlisted Securities Premium
d) Union Secondary Picketing **(1 mark)**

Score /5

B

Answer all parts of all questions.

1 Tick the three tasks that are normally dealt with by a firm's Marketing department.

a) Looking after all staff ☐ b) Paying bills ☐
c) Promoting people ☐ d) Promoting goods ☐
e) Buying new machinery ☐ f) Arranging an advertising campaign ☐
g) Carrying out quality control ☐ h) Undertaking market research ☐ **(3 marks)**

2 Select the one alternative that best fits the following sentences.
a) Market segmentation helps a business to target/tariff/test/try its market.
b) When a firm concentrates on one market segment only, it is trading in a narrow/national/net/niche market. An example of such a business is *Marks and Spencer/Vauxhall/The Sock Shop.*
c) A marketing department will link a firm's people to consumers/performance to costs/production to consumption/profits to capital.
(6 marks)

3 Match each product with the segmentation it best illustrates.
(Note: the product may fit more than one type of segmentation.)

Segmentation by:
a) Age
b) Income
c) Sex

Product
i) Expensive jewellery
ii) 'Own-brand' foodstuffs
iii) Clothes made for young boys
iv) Women's perfume
v) Membership of an exclusive gym

(5 marks)

Score /14

C

These are GCSE-style questions. Answer all parts of the questions. Continue on a separate sheet where necessary.

1 **Explain, using illustrations from UK business, what is meant by 'market'.**

....

....

.... **(3 marks)**

2 ***Freeze Ltd*** **makes ice-cream, which it sells direct to supermarket chains and freezer centres in the UK, not to the general public.** ***Freeze Ltd*** **is planning to market a new luxury ice-cream.**

a) Assess the importance of market segmentation to *Freeze Ltd*.

....

....

.... **(6 marks)**

b) Outline briefly an appropriate marketing strategy for the new luxury ice-cream.

....

....

....

....

....

....**(12 marks)**

3 ***Cartwright Ltd*****, a garage, sells vehicles to individuals and business customers. Explain how these different market segment groups might influence** ***Cartwright Ltd's*** **marketing.**

....

....

....

.... **(8 marks)**

Score /29

For more on this topic see pages 78–79 of your Success Guide.

Total score /48

How well did you do? ✗ 0–9 Try again 10–24 Getting there 25–37 Good work 38–48 Excellent! ✓

Market research

A

Choose just one answer: a, b, c or d.

1 Before starting to sell its existing goods in a new market, a business normally carries out:

a) new product development
b) market research
c) insurance
d) industrial action (1 mark)

2 Using figures and other numerical information is an example of:

a) qualitative data
b) quality control
c) queuing theory
d) quantitative research (1 mark)

3 An example of statistics published by the government is:

a) Economic Trends
c) Equal Pay Act
b) Directors' Report
d) The Financial Times (1 mark)

4 A group of respondents to a market research survey is called a:

a) sales campaign
b) span of control
c) sample
d) segment (1 mark)

5 The people who meet to discuss a firm's products are known as a consumer:

a) credit
b) durable
c) panel
d) profile (1 mark)

Score /5

B

Answer all parts of all questions.

1 Tick the two examples of primary ('field') research in the following list.

a) Trade magazines ☐
b) Telephone polls ☐
c) Surveys ☐
d) Government statistics ☐
e) Information from a book ☐

(2 marks)

2 Explain the difference between market research and marketing research.

....

.... (4 marks)

3 Which of the following statements are correct?

	Yes	No
a) Postal surveys are usually more expensive than face-to-face interviews	☐	☐
b) Primary data is collected just for the firm in question	☐	☐
c) Sales and production figures are examples of desk research	☐	☐
d) Secondary data is usually more expensive to obtain than primary data	☐	☐

(4 marks)

Score /10

C These are GCSE-style questions. Answer all parts of the questions. Continue on a separate sheet where necessary.

1 a) Outline the role and importance of market research to the national retailer *Tesco*.

....

.... **(4 marks)**

b) Explain whether a small company supplying clothes to *Tesco* will also need to carry out market research.

....

.... **(4 marks)**

2 **Sandra makes small wooden ornaments. She is planning to lease a small shop to sell these ornaments. Sandra wants to discover whether there is a large enough market for her products.**

a) Explain how market research could assist Sandra in discovering the nature of her local market.

....

....

.... **(4 marks)**

Sandra has gathered the following market research information about her customers: their age, their income, and their occupation.

b) i) What other market research information would be of use to Sandra?

....

....

.... **(4 marks)**

ii) How could Sandra obtain this information?

....

....

....

.... **(6 marks)**

Score /22

For more on this topic see pages 80–81 of your Success Guide.

Total score /37

How well did you do? 0–6 Try again 7–17 Getting there 18–29 Good work 30–37 Excellent!

Product

A

Choose just one answer: a, b, c or d.

1 The variety of goods or services offered by a business is known as its:
a) final accounts
b) trading policy
c) product range
d) contract of employment **(1 mark)**

2 Many larger retailers sell:
a) 'own-capital' goods
b) 'owner' goods
c) 'own-brand' goods
d) 'own-profit' goods **(1 mark)**

3 In the 'Boston Box', products with a low market share in a low-growth market are called:
a) Stars b) Cash Cows
c) Problem Children d) Dogs **(1 mark)**

4 Businesses try to lengthen the life of their products by using:
a) extension strategies
b) external strategies
c) enterprise strategies
d) employment strategies **(1 mark)**

5 Customers who buy the same item regularly show:
a) brand standing
b) brand leadership
c) brand loyalty
d) brand accounting **(1 mark)**

Score /5

B

Answer all parts of all questions.

1 Is the product life-cycle chart labelled correctly? Correct any errors on the graph itself.

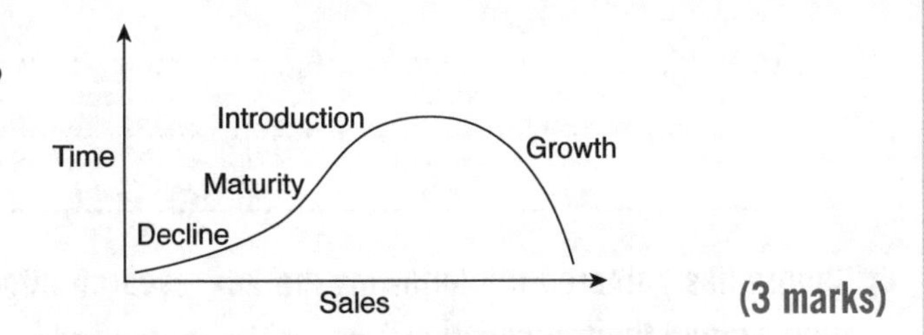

(3 marks)

2 Draw four arrows to link each part of the product life-cycle with the most appropriate section of the 'Boston Box'.

Product life-cycle	**'Boston Box'**
Introduction	Cash Cow
Growth	Dog
Maturity	Problem Child
Decline	Star

(4 marks)

3 The managers of *Shoes Ltd* have decided to launch a new sports shoe. Their ideas include:
a) Make the shoes in a range of bright colours
b) Advertise them using leaflets
c) Start selling them at a low price
d) Buy one, get a second pair half-price
e) Use Velcro instead of laces

Identify which of the above ideas would feature under the heading 'Product'. **(2 marks)**

Score /9

C

These are GCSE-style questions. Answer all parts of the questions. Continue on a separate sheet where necessary.

1 a) Explain why product branding is important to businesses.

....

....

.... **(6 marks)**

b) Large companies such as *Virgin* are using their brand names on more and more different goods and services. Outline the advantages and disadvantages to the company of doing this.

....

....

.... **(6 marks)**

BILL'S BRANDS – YOU KNOW THEY'RE GOOD

BILL'S BRANDS PURE ORANGE

BILL'S BISCUITS

BILL'S CHOCOLATE

BILL'S CHOCOLATE

2 a) Explain why creating new products is important to businesses.

....

.... **(4 marks)**

b) Using appropriate examples, analyse how businesses differentiate their products.

....

....

....

.... **(8 marks)**

Score /24

For more on this topic see pages 82–83 of your Success Guide.

Total score /38

How well did you do? 0–6 Try again 7–17 Getting there 18–29 Good work 30–38 Excellent!

Price

A

Choose just one answer: a, b, c or d.

1 The tactic of setting prices such as 99p or £9.95 is called:
a) prediction pricing
b) personal pricing
c) physical pricing
d) psychological pricing **(1 mark)**

2 Setting a product's price by adding an amount for profit to its cost figure is known as:
a) margin b) mark-up
c) monopoly d) merchandising **(1 mark)**

3 The 'law' of supply and demand states that:
a) price increases when demand and supply are the same
b) demand falls as price increases
c) supply falls when price increases
d) price stays the same when demand falls
(1 mark)

4 Penetration pricing sets:
a) a high price to gain high profits
b) different prices in different markets
c) prices lower than the cost of the product
d) a low price to gain a high market share
(1 mark)

5 A 'price leader' is another term for:
a) a price maker
b) a price taker
c) the price mechanism
d) price elasticity **(1 mark)**

Score /5

B

Answer all parts of all questions.

1 Complete the sentences by choosing the appropriate word from the box below.

If the price of a product is not right, ... will buy products sold by .... Lost customers mean lost .... for the business, and this in turn means lost ....

contracts	customers	competitors	consumables	policies	revenue
personnel	profits	recruitment	partnerships	recycling	retail

(4 marks)

2 Complete the table by matching a pricing method to the advantage or disadvantage given. The methods are: Skimming, Cost plus, and Penetration.

Feature	Method
a) This method ensures that all costs will be covered	....
b) Sales are maximised by this method	....
c) This method can lead to economies of sale	....
d) With this method, price falls when competitors enter the market	....
e) High prices can be set to make high profits with this method	....
f) This method assumes all goods will be sold	....

(6 marks)

Score /10

C

These are GCSE-style questions. Answer all parts of the questions. Continue on a separate sheet where necessary.

1 **The managers of *The Xclusive Hotel*, a luxury hotel in a city centre, are concerned about the low number of rooms being booked by visiting tourists. The hotel has to compete with lower-priced tourist hotels in its area. The managers are thinking of reducing room prices in order to compete with the tourist hotels.**

Explain the advantages and disadvantages of using this method to improve room occupancy and profits at the hotel.

....

....

....

.... **(8 marks)**

2 ***Finepans Ltd* is in the highly competitive kitchen equipment market. The company has developed a new range of cooking pans. This range was very costly to develop because it has a new 'high-tech' non-stick coating for the pans.**

a) Name three pricing strategies that *Finepans Ltd* should consider.

....

.... **(3 marks)**

b) Select one of these strategies as the most suitable in this situation. Justify your choice.

....

....

.... **(6 marks)**

c) 'Pricing products involves balancing being profitable with being competitive.' To what extent is this statement accurate?

....

....

.... **(5 marks)**

Score /22

For more on this topic see pages 84–85 of your Success Guide.

Total score /37

How well did you do? 0–7 Try again 8–17 Getting there 18-29 Good work 30–37 Excellent!

Place

A

Choose just one answer: a, b, c or d.

1 A company's products are sold by mail order. This is a:
a) distribution target
b) distribution of income
c) distribution plan
d) distribution channel **(1 mark)**

2 Breaking bulk is a service offered by wholesalers mainly to:
a) manufacturers
b) consumers
c) retailers
d) partners **(1 mark)**

3 Direct selling takes place from:
a) manufacturer to consumer
b) wholesaler to retailer
c) consumer to manufacturer
d) manufacturer to retailer **(1 mark)**

4 An important influence on the channel of distribution used is the:
a) cost of the premises
b) speed of the internet
c) scale of the business
d) qualifications of the staff **(1 mark)**

5 'Producer' is an alternative term for:
a) wholesaler
b) manufacturer
c) retailer
d) consumer **(1 mark)**

Score /5

B

Answer all parts of all questions.

1 Which of these channels of distribution is not correct?
a) Retailer → Producer → Wholesaler
b) Producer → Retailer → Consumer
c) Producer → Wholesaler → Consumer **(1 mark)**

2 Select the correct options from the pairs below.
a) E-commerce is becoming increasingly popular with businesses because:
i) consumers can buy products easily using the internet
ii) credit card fraud can't occur over the internet.
b) A problem of marketing through the internet is that:
i) it can be accessed 24 hours every day
ii) potential consumers may not be aware of the business's website. **(2 marks)**

Score /3

C

These are GCSE-style questions. Answer all parts of the questions. Continue on a separate sheet where necessary.

1 ***FoodFare Ltd*, a large food processor (manufacturer) based in the Midlands, supplies *Fine Foods Ltd*, a chain of supermarkets in the Midlands, with some of the food that it sells.**

Distribution channels have traditionally been:

Manufacturer → Wholesaler → Retailer → Consumer

a) What channel of distribution is used by *FoodFare Ltd*?

.... **(1 mark)**

b) Explain one advantage to *FoodFare Ltd* of using this channel.

.... **(2 marks)**

c) List three costs closely linked with distributing goods.

....

....

.... **(3 marks)**

2 ***Tastysweets plc* started as a small business, making and selling home-made chocolates in local shops. As the business grew, the owners noticed a change in people's buying habits, and as a result started selling directly to larger shops and supermarkets. The company now also sells direct to wholesalers and uses agents to sell its products to major hotel groups in the UK.**

a) Describe the change in *Tastysweets plc's* channels of distribution.

.... **(2 marks)**

b) Explain why these channels of distribution are likely to have changed as the company has grown.

....

.... **(4 marks)**

3 **Jennie has a market stall and sells products such as dog leads and collars, and toys for cats and dogs to pet lovers. Jennie is hoping to start selling these using the Internet. She plans to set up her own web page.**

a) Explain the advantages to Jennie of using the Internet to sell these products.

....

.... **(4 marks)**

b) Describe the main problems that Jennie is likely to face in this area.

....

.... **(4 marks)**

Score /20

For more on this topic see pages 86–87 of your Success Guide.

Total score /28

How well did you do? ✗ 0–6 Try again 7–14 Getting there 15–20 Good work 21–28 Excellent! ✓

Promoting by advertising

A

Choose just one answer: a, b, c or d.

1 Informative advertising sets out to:
a) tempt people to buy the firm's products
b) make people believe they need the firm's products
c) encourage competition between businesses
d) give information to people **(1 mark)**

2 Businesses advertise their goods and services in order to:
a) compete with other businesses
b) cooperate with other businesses
c) merge with other businesses
d) work with other businesses **(1 mark)**

3 Advertising is often linked with:
a) picketing
b) patents
c) packaging
d) productivity **(1 mark)**

4 A disadvantage of advertising in magazines compared with advertising on TV is:
a) more information can normally be given
b) the advert can be cut out and kept
c) there is no sound or movement
d) specialist groups can more easily be targeted **(1 mark)**

5 The person most likely to be responsible for advertising is the:
a) Chief Accountant
b) Production Director
c) Human Resources Director
d) Marketing Director **(1 mark)**

Score /5

B

Answer all parts of all questions.

1 Complete the following sentences by selecting the appropriate phrases from the box below.

Because television advertising is .... form, the larger companies tend to use it. It creates .... through its .... Alternative media, such as newspapers, allow readers to .... because it is in .... , unlike TV. Local radio is often used nowadays: it is .... than TV, but it has ....

keep a copy of the advert	a smaller audience	use of movement and sound	
the most expensive	a permanent form	great impact	less expensive

(7 marks)

2 Identify these arguments as either for or against advertising.

a) Unsuccessful advertising may lead to higher prices. For/Against
b) Advertising creates employment in its industry. For/Against
c) Advertising encourages competition, which lowers prices. For/Against
d) Advertising provides information for consumers. For/Against
e) Advertising tempts people to buy items they don't need. For/Against

(5 marks)

Score /12

C

These are GCSE-style questions. Answer all parts of the questions. Continue on a separate sheet where necessary.

1 ***Thomas Ltd*** **transfers silent movies onto DVD format. These are sold to its target audience.**

a) Define the term 'target audience'.

....

.... **(2 marks)**

b) Name two appropriate advertising media that *Thomas Ltd* might use. Explain why each is appropriate.

....

....

....

.... **(6 marks)**

c) *Thomas Ltd* also manufactures blank CDs, which are sold to retailers. Analyse whether *Thomas Ltd* should use the same advertising media to help sell these products.

....

.... **(4 marks)**

2 **The directors of** ***Fixx Ltd*** **wish to employ more staff to work in the company's new Internet Sales section.**

a) Select one method of advertising for the new staff. Justify your choice.

.... **(2 marks)**

b) *Fixx Ltd* sells a variety of glues and other solvents for DIY use. Discuss whether the Internet is an appropriate method to advertise these products.

....

....

.... **(4 marks)**

Score /18

For more on this topic see pages 88–89 of your Success Guide.

Total score /35

How well did you do? 0–6 Try again 7–16 Getting there 17–26 Good work 27–35 Excellent!

Other types of promotion

A

Choose just one answer: a, b, c or d.

1 An after-sales service offered by a garage to a customer who buys a car is:
a) free MOT tests when the car is serviced
b) arranging the loan to buy the car
c) promoting its New Year sales in the local paper
d) repairing the forecourt where cars are displayed **(1 mark)**

2 'POS' stands for:
a) performance of staff
b) product or service
c) price of shares
d) point of sale **(1 mark)**

3 'PR' is an abbreviation for:
a) press release
b) public relations
c) profit ratio
d) product range **(1 mark)**

4 The 'D' in 'AIDA' refers to:
a) creating a desire to own a product
b) carrying out a distribution of the products
c) having a dispute with a customer
d) creating a display for a product **(1 mark)**

5 Money-off offers, free gifts and competitions are examples of:
a) product portfolios
b) promotion incentives
c) pricing methods
d) persuasive advertising **(1 mark)**

Score /5

B

Answer all parts of all questions.

1 Match each term with the correct description.

Term	Description
a) Personal selling	i) Promotion that often uses sports events
b) Merchandising	ii) Using 'junk mail'
c) Sponsorship	iii) Face-to-face contact
d) Direct marketing	iv) Issuing press releases
e) Public relations	v) Point-of-sale displays
f) After-sales service	vi) Guarantees

(6 marks)

2 Place the following phrases in the correct order.
a) Action – buy the product
b) Interest – create this in the product
c) Attention – capture this
d) Desire – to own the product

Free Prize Draw

(4 marks)

Score /10

C These are GCSE-style questions. Answer all parts of the questions. Continue on a separate sheet where necessary.

1 ***Melody Ltd*** **used to sell music tapes by mail order. The owners now run a number of shops selling music, videos, DVDs and computer games. A new shop is opening in two weeks.**

Suggest and justify two promotional methods, other than advertising, that the owners should use to promote the new shop.

....

.... **(4 marks)**

2 ***Samson Ltd*** **makes machinery that is used by other companies.** ***Samson Ltd*** **sells these machines by using personal selling.**

a) Explain why personal selling is an appropriate technique for companies such as *Samson Ltd.*

....

.... **(4 marks)**

b) Describe one drawback to *Samson Ltd* of using personal selling.

.... **(2 marks)**

NEW & USED CARS

3 ***Shedd Ltd*** **has bought a new car dealership. The Marketing Manager must plan how topromote car sales. Name two appropriate sales promotion methods that the Marketing Manager may use. In each case explain why the Marketing Manager might choose to use them.**

....

....

....

.... **(4 marks)**

4 a) What is 'public relations'?

.... **(2 marks)**

b) Describe how a business is likely to use public relations.

....

.... **(3 marks)**

Score /19

For more on this topic see pages 90–91 of your Success Guide.

Total score /34

How well did you do? 0–6 Try again 7–16 Getting there 17–26 Good work 27–34 Excellent!

GCSE-style practice paper

Little Feet Ltd is a company that makes and sells children's shoes. These shoes are recognised as being high quality and are expensive to buy. *Little Feet Ltd* sells these shoes to *Booties plc*, a large retailer with stores in many towns.

Johnny and Natalie Osborne established *Little Feet Ltd* several years ago as a partnership. Johnny and Natalie are now directors of the company and employ over 30 staff to make the shoes. *Little Feet Ltd* has three main departments: Production (with Johnny in charge), Marketing, where Natalie acts as the Marketing Director and is assisted by a Sales Manager, and Finance. They also employ a Human Resources Officer.

The shoes in the company's popular *CosyToes* range are made from leather, although Johnny – the Production Director – is examining whether the company should switch to using man-made materials. The employees in the Production Department, who are all members of the same trade union, would prefer to continue using leather to make shoes, since they are trained in its use, and are suspicious of the proposed new materials.

Use the above information, where relevant, in answering the questions that follow.

1 Complete each of these sentences using the correct word or phrase.

a) *Little Feet Ltd* is based in the .... sector of the economy.

private public mixed

b) *Little Feet Ltd* is owned by ....

directors employees shareholders

c) *Little Feet Ltd* adds a percentage to the amount it costs to make a pair of shoes.

This is called a ....

margin mark-up bonus

d) If *Little Feet Ltd* moved to a new site, this would be called ....

relocation distribution promotion

e) *Little Feet Ltd* pays its suppliers by using ....

invoices statements cheques

(5 marks)

2 a) Explain how Johnny and Natalie have changed the form of ownership of *Little Feet Ltd.*

....

....

.... **(4 marks)**

b) Describe **one** advantage to Johnny and Natalie as a result of making this change.

....

.... **(2 marks)**

c) Explain fully the difference between the present form of ownership of *Little Feet Ltd* and that of *Booties plc.*

....

....

....

....

....

.... **(8 marks)**

3 **Name, justifying your selection, an appropriate method of payment for the:**

a) production staff

....

....

.... **(5 marks)**

b) Human Resources Officer.

....

....

.... **(5 marks)**

4 **Natalie would like to enter the mass market for children's shoes. She believes, however, that *Little Feet Ltd* cannot compete successfully with the businesses that dominate the mass market for children's shoes.**

Explain why Natalie is likely to be correct in her belief.

....

....

....

....

.... **(6 marks)**

5 **Johnny wants to try entering the mass market for children's shoes. This is a very competitive market, so Johnny has decided to produce a small range of non-leather shoes for this market. The company will need to invest in new machinery.**

a) Explain how his decision will affect the work of the:

i) Human Resources Officer

....

....

....

.... **(6 marks)**

ii) Sales Manager.

....

....

....

.... **(6 marks)**

b) Suggest **one** pricing strategy for these new shoes. Justify your choice.

....

....

.... **(4 marks)**

c) Explain how the production staff's trade union is likely to deal with their concern about using the new materials.

....

....

....

....

....

.... **(8 marks)**

6 **If the new range of shoes is produced, describe the benefits from two likely economies of scale for *Little Feet Ltd.***

....

....

....

....

....

.... **(8 marks)**

7 Gary Fitzpatrick the Finance Manager, has produced the break-even chart below for the new line of shoes. These shoes are to be sold at £20 each.

a) Complete the following table:

Number of pairs of shoes	0	1000	2000	3000	4000	5000
Fixed costs (£)	50000					
Variable costs (£)	0	7500				
Total costs (£)	50000					
Total Revenue (£)						

(8 marks)

b) Complete the break-even chart by:

i) plotting the total revenue line

ii) labelling the other lines

iii) identifying the break-even output.

(7 marks)

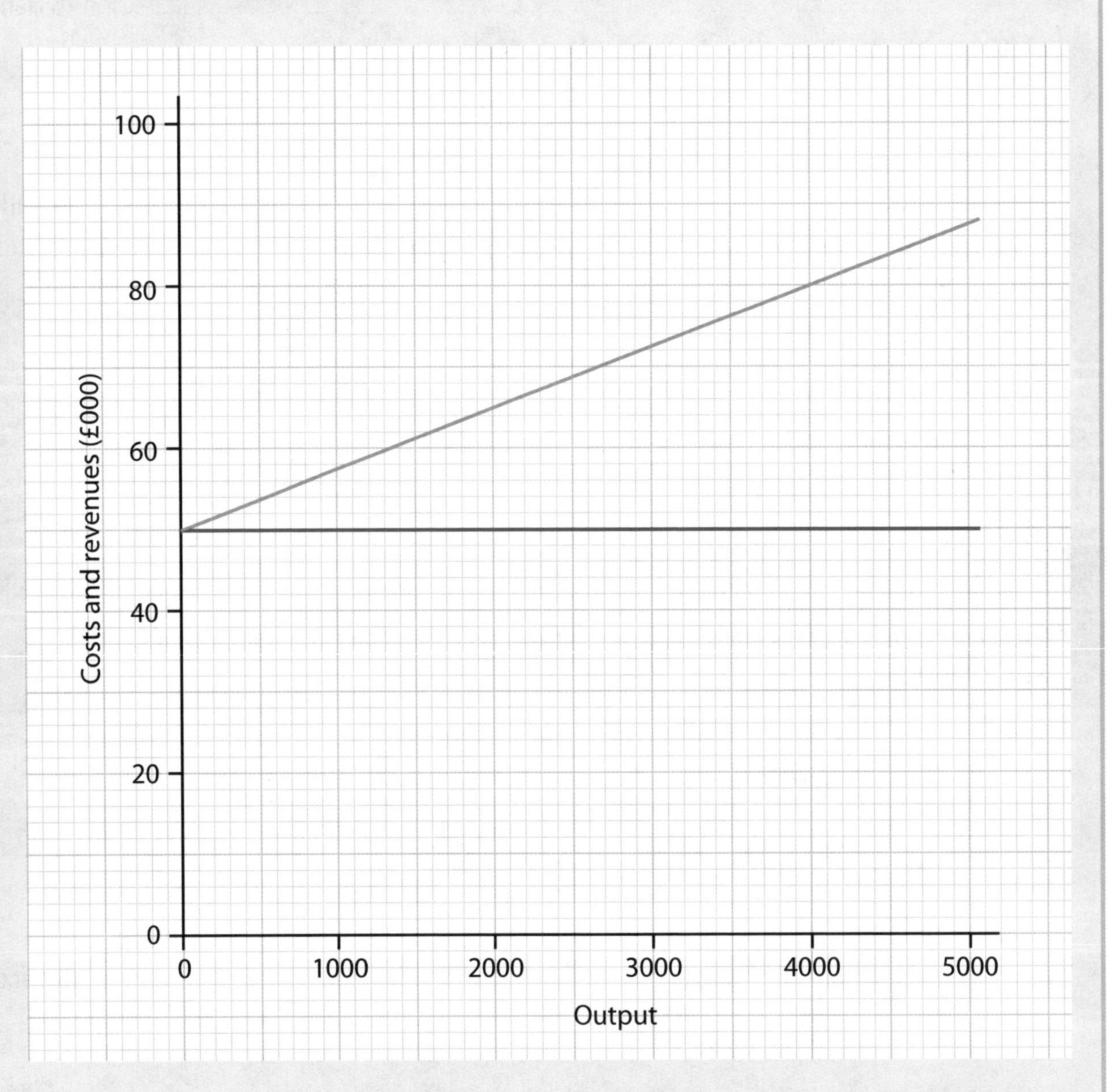

8 **Gary Fitzpatrick has also produced the following financial information for *Little Feet Ltd*.**

	This year	Last year
Sales	£400000	£360000
Net profit	£80000	£72000
Fixed assets	£160000	£150000
Current assets	£60000	£50000
Current liabilities	£40000	£50000
Capital	£180000	£150000

Calculate and comment on the following ratios for both years:

a) net profit percentage

....

....

....

....

b) return on capital

....

....

....

....

c) current ratio.

....

....

....

.... **(12 marks)**

9 **Gary will have to arrange additional finance to obtain more machines if the new shoes are to be made. Describe and justify one source, other than investing new capital, for the new machines.**

....

....

....

....

.... **(6 marks)**

Total for paper: 100 marks

Practice paper answers

1 a) private
b) shareholders
c) mark-up
d) relocation
e) cheques.

2 a) The ownership has changed from a partnership, an unincorporated business, to a limited company (an incorporated business). Johnny and Natalie are now separate from *Little Feet Ltd*, which can enter contracts and take legal action in its own name.

b) Limited liability: Johnny and Natalie are no longer personally responsible for any business debts that *Little Feet Ltd* cannot meet.

c) *Little Feet Ltd* and *Booties plc* are both limited companies with shareholders as owners and directors as controllers, but *Little Feet Ltd* is a private company, and *Booties plc* is a public company. This means that *Little Feet Ltd* is better able to keep its financial affairs private, although it cannot approach the public directly to obtain capital, unlike *Booties plc*. *Little Feet Ltd* is less likely to face a hostile takeover bid because its voting shares are not being traded on a stock market.

3 a) Piece-rate wage: this will encourage the staff to work hard, because they are paid on the basis of the number of pairs of shoes they make. However, Johnny will need to check that the quality of the shoes is being maintained and that staff are not rushing production.

b) Fixed salary: an annual amount divided into 12 equal monthly amounts. A fixed salary is normally expected for such a post, and commission or bonuses are not normally given since there are few measurable targets that this person can be set (unless it is to reduce labour turnover, when the Officer could be awarded a bonus).

4 *Little Feet Ltd* is a relatively small company (just over 30 staff are employed). It therefore does not gain from economies of scale at present, unlike larger businesses. Also, the larger businesses will have advanced production and distribution networks, with which *Little Feet Ltd* cannot compete. Since *Little Feet Ltd's* existing products (quality shoes) are aimed at a niche market rather than a mass market, the company will not have appropriate marketing or finance systems in place to compete.

5 a) i) The Human Resources Officer may need to arrange training for the production staff in new techniques. Other staff may also need training, e.g. in dealing with new customers. The Officer will also need to deal with any problems arising from the production workers' concerns.

ii) The Sales Manager will need to change existing advertising and promotion, and/or create new advertising and promotion, because of the new line and new market. The Manager will also need to work with others, e.g. advising the Finance Manager on pricing, and the Human Resources Officer on additional training requirements for sales staff.

b) Penetration pricing. The company will be a price taker, not a price maker, because it is a newcomer to a market where prices are very competitive. As a result, it cannot set a high price and expect to sell the new range.

c) The union representatives are likely first to discuss matters with the Human Resources Officer, expressing the concerns of their members. If the production staff accept working with the new materials, the union representatives may try to negotiate new pay and working conditions. If the staff find working with the new materials unacceptable, the union may arrange to take industrial action. Possible action to take includes the following: banning overtime, which could cause problems in meeting production targets; work-to-rule, where staff make shoes following all rules 'to the letter'; and strikes, where staff withdraw their labour.

6 Technical economies: the company is investing in new machinery, which is likely to make production more efficient. Marketing economies: if the company is successful, more expensive marketing methods may be used, but this extra cost is spread over a much larger output, making it cheaper when calculated per pair of shoes.

7 a)

Number of pairs of shoes	0	1000	2000	3000	4000	5000
Fixed costs (£)	50000	50000	50000	50000	50000	50000
Variable costs (£)	0	7500	15000	22500	30000	37500
Total costs (£)	50000	57500	65000	72500	80000	87500
Total revenue (£)	0	20000	40000	60000	80000	100000

b)

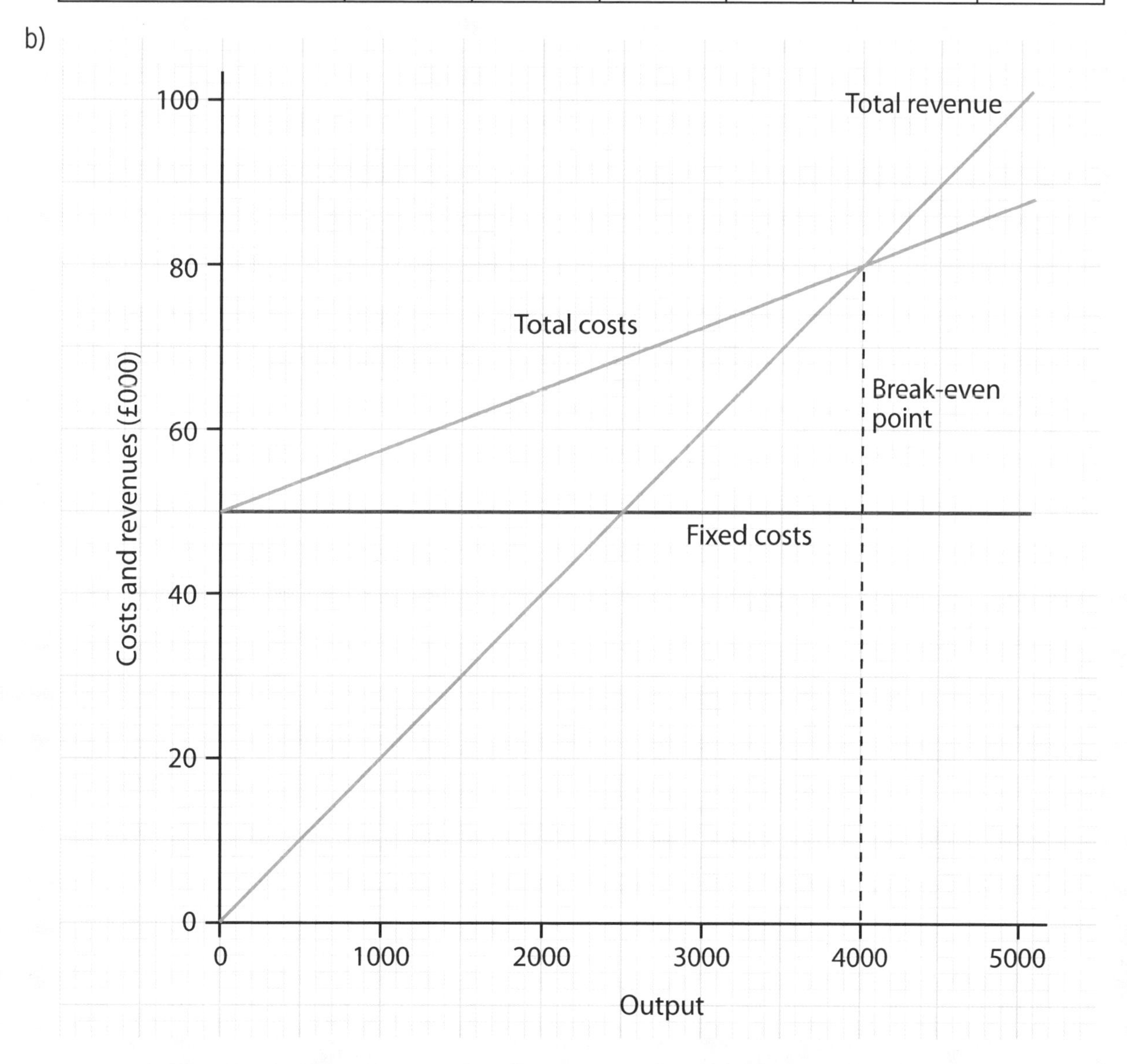

8 (This year's figures first):

a) 20%, 20%*. This ratio indicates the amount of net profit per £1 sales made. There has been no change, even though sales have increased, so the company has done well to keep its profit margin the same.

b) 44.4%, 48%**. This ratio shows the profitability or otherwise of Johnny and Natalie's investment. This return has dropped, because capital has increased proportionally more than net profit: it is still a very high return for Johnny and Natalie.

c) 1.5 to 1, 1 to 1***. This ratio indicates how 'liquid' the company is. The current ratio is higher this year, so the company seems to have sufficient funds to 'pay its way'.

* Workings: £80 000 as a percentage of £400 000; £72 000 as a percentage of £360 000.
** Workings: £80 000 as a percentage of £180 000; £72 000 as a percentage of £150 000.
*** Workings: £60 000 divided by £40 000; £50 000 divided by £50 000.

9 Bank loan. This is likely to be available, since the company is profitable (see above answer). The bank may want the loan secured against the company's fixed assets, and Gary can offer this as security for the loan. The bank will state a rate of interest, and a length of time for the loan, and this will help Gary budget for the cost of the loan and its repayment.